MALAYSIA

WESTVIEW PROFILES · NATIONS OF CONTEMPORARY ASIA
Mervyn Adams Seldon, Series Editor

Malaysia: Tradition, Modernity, and Islam,
R. S. Milne and Diane K. Mauzy

Laos: Keystone of Indochina, Arthur J. Dommen

Bangladesh: A New Nation in an Old Setting, Craig Baxter

Pakistan: A Nation in the Making, Shahid Javed Burki

Sri Lanka: Portrait of an Island Republic, Tissa Fernando

† *Vietnam: Nation in Revolution,* William J. Duiker

† *The Philippines: A Singular and A Plural Place,*
David Joel Steinberg

Burma: A Socialist Nation of Southeast Asia, David I. Steinberg

† *Japan: Profile of a Postindustrial Power,* Ardath W. Burks

Nepal: Profile of a Himalayan Kingdom,
Leo E. Rose and John T. Scholz

Thailand, Charles F. Keyes

Also of Interest

Malaysia: Economic Expansion and National Unity, John Gullick

Conflict and Violence in Singapore and Malaysia, 1945–1983,
Richard Clutterbuck

*Swamp Rice Farming: The Indigenous Pahang Malay
Agricultural System,* Donald H. Lambert

The Armed Forces in Contemporary Asian Societies,
edited by Edward A. Olsen and Stephen Jurika, Jr.

Southeast Asia Divided: The ASEAN-Indochina Crisis,
edited by Donald E. Weatherbee

† *An Atlas of South Asia,* Ashok K. Dutt and Margaret Geib

† *Southeast Asia: Realm of Contrasts,* Third Revised Edition,
edited by Ashok K. Dutt

† Available in hardcover and paperback.

About the Book and Authors

Malaysia has many problems in common with other developing countries—including the difficult task of achieving economic progress and modernization while retaining useful traditional values, reducing poverty, and minimizing dependence on the export of a few primary products. It also has a remarkable, if not unique, diversity of cultures. Its ethnic divisions (approximately 47 percent Malay, 34 percent Chinese, 9 percent Indian, and 10 percent "other") are deep, reflecting differences in race, language, culture, and religion. At present, the main danger of serious ethnic tension arises from the impact of the Islamic resurgence. The Malays, who are dominant politically, are Muslims, but very few Chinese, the second largest ethnic group, are Muslims. It is especially remarkable, given this ethnic mix, that Malaya (which became Malaysia in 1963) achieved independence peacefully (in 1957), has experienced no military coups or takeovers, and has regularly held elections. This book examines Malaysia's history, population, social structure, politics, and economics as well as its climate, agriculture, and wildlife and seeks to explain why, despite its inherent ethnic tensions, Malaysia has survived and even prospered.

R. S. Milne is a professor emeritus of political science at the University of British Columbia. He has written and edited more than a dozen books and is a fellow of the Royal Society of Canada. **Diane K. Mauzy** is a lecturer in the department of political science, University of British Columbia. She has published a number of books and articles on politics in Malaysia and is editor of *Politics in the ASEAN States* (1984).

MALAYSIA

Tradition, Modernity, and Islam

R. S. Milne
and
Diane K. Mauzy

Westview Press / Boulder and London

Westview Profiles/Nations of Contemporary Asia

Published in 1986 in the United States of America by Westview Press, Inc.; Frederick A. Praeger, Publisher; 5500 Central Avenue, Boulder, Colorado 80301

Library of Congress Cataloging-in-Publication Data
Milne, R. S. (Robert Stephen), 1919–
  Malaysia: tradition, modernity, and Islam.
  (Westview profiles. Nations of contemporary Asia)
  Bibliography: p.
  Includes index.
  1. Malaysia. I. Mauzy, Diane K., 1942–
II. Title. III. Series.
DS592.M53 1986   959.5   85-17803
ISBN 0-8133-0011-8

Printed and bound in the United States of America

The paper used in this publication meets the minimum requirements of the American National Standard for Permanence of Paper for Printed Library Materials Z39.48-1984.

10   9   8   7   6   5   4   3   2   1

To Fala,
whose help increased by leaps and bounds

Contents

Illustrations

Preface

This book is intended principally for the general reader and for students who may wish later to become more specialized. Footnotes have been kept to a minimum, but further references may be found in our other publications, which are listed in the bibliography.

The book is not the product of any special research, but is based on over twenty years of research experience and writing about Malaysia. Our most recent visit (1984) confirmed that it is a fascinating, important, agreeable, and rewarding country in which to conduct research.

It would be inappropriate to express our thanks by name to the hundreds of politicians, journalists, academics, businesspeople, and others or to the dozens of foundations, universities, and libraries that have helped us. However, we must acknowledge the assistance of those who have contributed to updating our information and providing illustrations for this book: Y. B. Datuk Rais Yatim, Minister of Information, Malaysia, for photographs and the Malaysian High Commission, Ottawa, for publications and photographs. We are also indebted to Grace Cross, Nancy Mina, and Petula Muller for typing the manuscript.

R.S.M.
D.K.M.

Special Terms and Concepts

In reading about any country, one is bound to encounter unfamiliar terms and ideas. As Malaysia is no exception, we seek to clarify the following:

1. Spelling.
2. The use and form of proper names.
3. Ranks and titles.
4. The distinction between "Malaysia"/"Malaysian" and "Malay."
5. Statistics.

Spelling

The spelling of words in Malay is not consistent because of recent substantial changes in the language (see Chapter 4). Many new words have been coined since independence, and a few years ago spellings were changed in the interests of achieving uniformity between *Bahasa Malaysia* and *Bahasa Indonesia.* Only a small proportion of those who use Malay are thoroughly aware of these developments, however. Consequently, variations are found in the spellings of even familiar words such as the names of the states (e.g., "Johore" or "Johor"). Hence there are limits to the degree of consistency in this book. The authors have tried to use new spellings except where they have failed to gain currency.

The Use and Form of Proper Names

It is sometimes difficult to figure out the accepted usage for Malay names. Malays are not referred to by their patronymic. Rather, they are referred to by their given name(s), and their fathers' names are attached at the end after "bin" (for males) or "binte" (for females). "Bin" and "binte" mean "by," similar to the Arabic "ibn." Moreover, some Malays have dropped the use of "bin/binte" (e.g., the third prime minister, Tun Hussein Onn, son of Dato Onn bin Jaafar). When there are two given names and the first is "Abdul," either the person is referred to by both given names (e.g., Abdul Rahman) or the "Abdul" is dropped (e.g., the second prime minister, Tun Razak—otherwise known as Tun Abdul Razak bin Dato Hussein). Similarly, as the first of two names, "Mohamed" (and its variations) is sometimes dropped.

Malaysia's Chinese use the traditional spelling and three names. Although dialect differences lead to some arbitrariness, in general Chinese names are simple and consistent. The family name is first and is followed by two given names. For example, in the name "Lim Kit Siang," "Lim" is the family name; friends would call him "Kit Siang." The only exception for Chinese names occurs when a person uses a Christian first name; then the family name appears last, as for the Chinese politician, Michael Chen, who would otherwise be known as Chen Wing Sum. Sometimes one finds a Christian first name, the family name, and then the Chinese given names.

Ranks and Titles

Some descendants of royalty have the title of "Tunku" or "Tengku" (Prince), which is spelled differently in different states. The word "Haji" or the feminine "Hajiah" in a name indicates that the person has made the pilgrimage to Mecca.

Nonhereditary titles may be conferred by a ruler or governor at the state level or by the *agung* at the federal level. In most cases the nomination would come from the appropriate minister. The most usual state title is "Dato" or "Datuk," which sometimes takes the longer form, as in "Datuk Seri" or "Datu Amar" (the feminine form is "Datin"). The federal equivalent is "Tan Sri." A higher federal rank, rarely conferred, is "Tun." Men without a title are referred to as "Encik" (Mr.). The feminine equivalent is "Che."

"Malaysia"/"Malaysian" and "Malay"

All citizens of Malaysia are Malaysians, but not all of them are Malays. The federal constitution defines a "Malay" partly with reference to behavior. A Malay is a person who habitually speaks Malay, professes the Muslim religion, and conforms to Malay custom. Moreover, to be Malay, a person must have been born (or have a parent who was born or domiciled at the time of independence in 1957) in the Federation of Malaya or in Singapore. Two qualifications are necessary. Some inhabitants of Sarawak and Sabah are known as Malays. In addition, persons who meet the above criteria are not recognized as Malays by the laws of the various states unless they also come from a "Malay" race. Popular use of the term "Malay" also employs ethnic origin as a criterion.

Statistics

The statistics in this book (mostly in Chapters 4 and 6) are taken mainly from official publications, in particular the Malaysia plans and their midterm reviews, which are published by the Malaysian government and constitute an essential basis for economic research. However, some of the statistics in these and other sources refer only to Peninsular Malaysia, not to all of Malaysia. The reader should therefore be careful to note which statistics apply to which area.

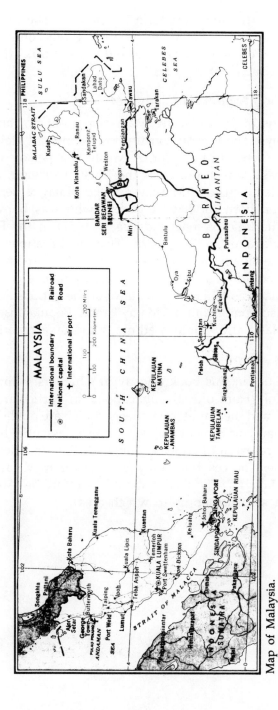

Map of Malaysia.

Source: U.S. Department of State, "Background Notes: Malaysia," October 1983.

1

Introduction

A few years ago one of the present authors, then in Malaysia, was approached by a visiting New Zealand Member of Parliament. "I have just two important questions for you," he said. "What is really going on in this country, and what are the names of the two main types of dress worn by Chinese women here?" In a way, this book is an answer to these questions. It does indeed attempt to explain "what is going on" in Malaysia. In addition, it tries to convey, through occasional invocations of the picturesque, something of the *feel* of the country.

Malaysia is a relatively new country, formed in 1963 from the union between the existing state of Malaya and the Borneo territories of Sabah (formerly known as British North Borneo) and Sarawak. All three had been under British colonial rule, Sarawak and Sabah until as late as 1963, although Malaya had already gained its independence, peacefully, in 1957. Singapore was also part of Malaysia from 1963 to 1965, but after mounting tensions it withdrew. Malaya's six-year experience of self-rule, combined with its larger population and greater degree of development, made it the leading partner in Malaysia. It contains the capital, Kuala Lumpur, where the important political and economic decisions are made. Hence, although this book tries to bring out something of the unique flavor of Sarawak and Sabah, inevitably the central focus is on Malaya, now referred to as Peninsular Malaysia.

Politically, Malaysia is remarkable because it is the only Southeast Asian country, apart from Singapore, that has held free elections at approximately regular intervals since its

1

independence. Unlike the armed forces in many neighboring countries, its military is clearly subordinate to the civil power and there has never been any threat of a military coup. It was decided that Malaya, and later Malaysia, should have a form of government resembling that of Britain, with a prime minister and a parliament. There was a problem, however: What was to become of the eleven component states of Malaya—Johor, Kedah, Kelantan, Melaka, Negeri Sembilan, Pahang, Penang, Perak, Perlis, Selangor, and Terengganu? Apart from Penang and Melaka, these states had hereditary rulers (mostly known as sultans), who had been retained (with mostly symbolic powers) when the British took over control. Which of them, all jealous of their rights and pre-rogatives, was to play the constitutional role corresponding to that of the British monarch? The solution adopted was that the rulers should choose one of their own number, in turn, to serve as king for a period of five years only. The existence of states and rulers also led to the adoption of a federal form of government, but with the states being allocated very limited powers. In 1963, when Malaysia was formed, Sarawak and Sabah were added to the list of states.

Geographically, Malaysia consists of two parts, separated by about 400 miles of open sea. One, Peninsular Malaysia, lies nearly at the tip of the landmass of Southeast Asia, with Thailand to the north and only the small state of Singapore, nearly on the equator, to the south. The other, consisting of Sarawak and Sabah, forms the northern quarter of the large island of Borneo. At one time these areas were referred to as West and East Malaysia, respectively. Malaysia is one of the smaller Southeast Asian states, with a population of about 15 million and an area of some 129,000 square miles, more than twice the size of Florida. Most of the people live in Peninsular Malaysia, although it is the smaller of the two components.

Peninsular Malaysia has an east and a west coastal plain, with a central mountain range rising to more than 7,000 feet in between. Sarawak and Sabah also feature a coastal plain, which is often swampy. The hills and mountains in the interior include Mount Kinabalu, which, at 13,500 feet, is the highest peak in Southeast Asia. The climate in Malaysia is tropical (i.e., humid throughout the year except in a few hilly areas), with temperatures ranging from 75 to 90 degrees. More than two-thirds of the area is covered by tropical rain forest. Rainfall, about 100 inches a year on the average, is at its highest during the two monsoon seasons, which occur at different times throughout the country.

The west coast of Peninsular Malaysia, except for the northern section, is more settled and developed than the east coast, primarily as a result of the exploitation of tin there during the nineteenth century. Much of the interior is jungle. There are several areas of settlement along the coasts of Sarawak and Sabah, but the interior has been less penetrated and less developed than that of Peninsular Malaysia, and agriculture often takes the form of shifting cultivation. Communications by road, rail, sea, and air are generally effective in, and among, the major areas of settlement. In Peninsular Malaysia they were greatly improved about twenty years ago, when the ferries that supplemented road links along the east coast were replaced by bridges. Between the west coast and Penang island a much longer bridge, claimed to be the third longest in the world, was opened in September 1985.

Before independence, Malaysia was dependent mainly on what the land could provide—on crops such as rice, rubber, and palm oil; on timber; and on minerals, principally tin. In the past, the location of crop-growing areas and minerals has been important in determining concentrations of population and sources of livelihood. Rubber, although planted throughout the country, tends to be concentrated in the southwest of Peninsular Malaysia, principally Johor and Negeri Sembilan. Increasingly, it is being replaced by the more profitable palm oil. Rice cultivation is practiced mainly in the four northern states of Peninsular Malaysia, with the aid of extensive (and expensive) irrigation—notably, the Muda scheme in Kedah. But in spite of these efforts, it is hard to make rice growing profitable. Some "dry" rice cultivation is still practiced in the hilly areas of Sarawak and Sabah. Timber reserves are greater in Sarawak and Sabah than in the whole of Peninsular Malaysia, because exploitation without much regard for conservation had begun earlier in the latter. Reserves are still substantial, however, in Pahang and Terengganu.

Among the minerals, tin deposits (now seriously depleted) are concentrated in central and southern Peninsular Malaysia, principally in Perak. Throughout the last decade, offshore oil discoveries have boosted the Malaysian economy. Reserves in Terengganu are somewhat larger than those in Sarawak and Sabah but were discovered later; thus, current production comes mostly from these two states. Natural-gas production has also become important in the last few years, the main source being in the Bintulu area (Sarawak). Manufacturing, too, has recently expanded, thus supplementing the other sources of wealth and leading to an increasing concentration of population in areas near the capital, Kuala Lumpur.

Malaysia's per capita gross national product (GNP) is surpassed in Southeast Asia only by the island state of Singapore and the tiny oil-rich state of Brunei. Malaysia is approaching the economic status of Singapore, which is recognized as falling into the category of "newly industrialized nations." Unfortunately, this designation does not mean that poverty is rare. Although many necessities, such as clothing and shelter, are more cheaply obtainable here than in North America or Western Europe, and although deaths from hunger are practically unknown, malnutrition does exist and the basic human needs of some people are left unsatisfied. This problem has been a prime concern of the government recently, as discussed in Chapter 6.

Another aspect of government policy is unusual. In 1969, following violent outbreaks in Kuala Lumpur, the government decided that the Malays, along with other indigenous inhabitants (sometimes collectively referred to as *bumiputra*, or sons of the soil) needed government help to overcome their economic backwardness. Such assistance was a principal objective of the government's "New Economic Policy." To comprehend how this policy came about, one must understand the ethnic composition of the population. The Malays and other indigenous groups, descended from ancestors who settled in the area about 4,000 years ago, make up just over half the population. The ancestors of the remainder, mostly Chinese but also including Indians, arrived later—at most, a few hundred years ago. In the other countries of Southeast Asia, the proportion of such "immigrant races" is much lower, except in Singapore, where the Chinese constitute a majority. Most Chinese and Indian immigration took place under British rule, principally to provide workers for tin mines and rubber estates, whereas the Malays remained almost exclusively peasants. Several features distinguished the Chinese and Indians from Malays: appearance, language, religion (all Malays but few Indians and even fewer Chinese are Muslims), and segregated areas of residence, as well as largely different occupations.

This residential and occupational segregation was quite a workable arrangement under British rule, but after independence it led to difficulties. How could there be national unity in a country with such a diverse population? What would be the effect of breaking down barriers between the ethnic groups, for example through urbanization? Would closer contacts lead to friction, inasmuch as the Chinese might despise the Malays as backward while the Malays would look upon the Chinese as "unclean" because they ate pork, which is forbidden by Islam? Were successive generations of Malays to remain mainly peasants while most traders were Chinese? Above all, who was to hold political power? The Malays, whose rulers had concluded treaties with the British, initially controlled the government after independence; but, if strict democratic rules were to operate, might not their dominance be threatened by higher Chinese and Indian birthrates? These questions will be answered in full later on. The point to remember now is that there were no easy solutions such as "assimilation." The ethnic cleavages were too deep. Even today, when there is rather more contact among the groups than before, and when language barriers are eroding, Islam constitutes a dividing line between Malays (and some other indigenous peoples) and the Chinese and Indian "non-Malays."

At present, the land, its products, and its wild creatures offer much to interest tourists, who now number about 3 million a year. To be sure, spectacular archaeological and architectural attractions are few; in these areas of interest

Malaysia cannot compete with Angkor Wat in Kampuchea or Borobudur in Indonesia. On the other hand, some Malaysian scenery is hard to surpass. The adventurous tourist can climb majestic Mount Kinabalu in Sabah, its peak surrounded by the clouds, or visit the "beach of passionate love" in Kelantan. Less strenuous is a stroll around historic George Town, Penang, although at present its appearance is being changed for the worse by "development." Melaka has an even earlier heritage of buildings, or their remains, from Portuguese and Dutch colonial days, as well as an actual settlement of the descendants of the Portuguese.

There are no huge game parks or organized safaris in Malaysia, unlike some parts of Africa. But several hundred tigers (the beast represented on Malaysia's crest) still exist, the numbers in each state constituting a good index of economic and social development. The last noncaptive tiger seen in Kuala Lumpur was swept helplessly through the town in the heavy floods of 1930. Elephants are protected by a conservation program but are chased away from settled areas. Early in 1984 an operation, almost military in its carefully planned logistics, was carried out in an effort to save an elephant herd that had been trapped on an island by the rising waters of a dam. A variety of Malaysian wild ox, the *banteng*, or *seladang*, is said to be the largest in the world. The orangutan (literally, "jungle man") originated in Borneo and is still found in Sabah. More accessible to tourists are Malaysia's fruits, including pineapples, mangoes, starfruits, mangosteens, guavas, papayas, and, above all, durians, although only pineapples are produced in any quantity for export. Durians, a decidedly acquired taste for foreigners, who first have to break through the "smell barrier," are madly sought after by Malaysians. In 1983, the state of Perak held a durian festival, and one of its towns even promoted a contest to find the best "durian opener" (although the outcome was inconclusive because the rules were not sufficiently defined).

Perhaps Malaysia deserves the phrase "instant Asia" more than Singapore, which coined the phrase. The Malaysian population includes not only Malays, Chinese, and Indians but also *orang asli* (aborigines, or "original people") and an extensive range of native ethnic groups in Sarawak and Sabah. So widespread are Malaysia's economic links with Japan that Japanese businessmen also constitute part of the show, to say nothing of the sometimes quaint groups of tourists from all over the world.

The varieties of dress, particularly those for women, are indeed spectacular; they include the tight-waisted Malay *sarong kebaya,* the Chinese *cheongsam* (the more glamorous of the two types of Chinese dress), and the Indian *sari,* as well as the attractive costumes worn in Sarawak and Sabah. The Islamic resurgence, however, has led some Malay women to adopt more sober garb, in the form of head-to-toe garments that reveal only the lower part of the face. Nevertheless, Malaysia's numerous festivals, whatever their effect on productivity, provide occasions for colorful dress—among them, the Prophet Muhammed's birthday, *Hari Raya Puasa* (the end of the Muslim fasting month), the Chinese New Year, *Deepavali* (the Hindu festival of lights), and several others.

Malay games and pastimes include *silat* (the ancient Malay art of self-defense); the skillful maneuvering of carefully crafted, eye-catching kites; top-spinning; and *sepak takraw,* a game resembling volleyball in which the use of hands or forearms is prohibited. Malay dances, such as *joget,* have been supplemented by dances from Sarawak and Sabah, such as the unusual Kadazan bird dance. One may also watch the Malay *wayang kulit* (traditional puppet theater) and the Chinese opera. Chinese funeral processions are rousing—indeed, deafening—affairs, and the weddings of all ethnic groups are colorful.

The foregoing features are attractive elements of Malaysian life, but the country also has its trouble spots. Its economic problems resemble those of other countries that have made considerable economic progress but are faced with rising economic expectations. As described in Chapter 6, these include such matters as (1) how best to concentrate on the most profitable agricultural crops with the use of appropriate technology, but without causing distress to peasants attached to traditional methods; (2) how to determine the most advantageous timing for launching new industrial ventures; (3) how to profit from the experience of more economically advanced countries, especially Japan; and, simultaneously, (4) how to fight poverty.

A controversy that surfaced in 1983–1984, but was at least temporarily resolved at that time, illustrates the tensions between traditional and modern elements in the society. The attempt to insert old-time rulers and the new office of king into a modern constitutional structure (see Chapter 5) led to problems because the rulers were not content to be restricted to a purely symbolic role.

Problems also arose due to Malaysia's unusual ethnic composition—in particular, the fact that the dominant Malays (and Muslims) only slightly outnumber the non-Malays. Unlike other predominantly Muslim countries with small ethnic minorities, the ruling Malays cannot allow the non-Malays to go their own way, nor is it feasible to assimilate them by force. Attainment of a degree of national unity has been complicated by the effects in Malaysia, as elsewhere, of the worldwide resurgence of Islam, which is the official religion of Malaysia, although the constitution guarantees freedom of worship for those who follow other religions. This issue has engaged much of the attention of Malaysia's leaders in the 1980s. On the other hand, the government has successfully tried to reduce the sharp divisions between Peninsular Malaysia and the geographically separated states of Sarawak and Sabah. These attempts were symbolized by the 1983 decision to standardize time zones in the two regions.

How can Islam be reconciled with the modernization process, and how can its values be promoted without alienating the non-Muslims? Even the issue of national security, which Malaysia shares with other countries, has ethnic aspects. Policy toward China cannot ignore the existence of the large population of Chinese descent, nor can dealings with Indonesia overlook the ties of race, religion, and language linking the two countries.

The complex and fascinating interactions of tradition, modernization (including economic development), and ethnicity, currently most prominent in the form of Islam, constitute the principal themes of this book.

2

Early History: Colonial Rule

Southeast Asia was settled over thousands of years' time by waves of migrants who originated in Mongolia and China. (The one exception was the earlier migration of Negritos from Melanesia and Polynesia, whose descendants in Malaysia are called *orang asli.*) The Proto-Malays, descendants of the Ibans and some of other tribal groups found in Sabah and Sarawak, migrated to the Malaysian region between 2500 and 1500 B.C., making them one of the earliest groups to arrive. They were followed by the ancestors of the present day Malays, the Deutero-Malays (coastal Malays), whose migration pushed the Proto-Malays into the interior and to more remote regions, such as Borneo. The Proto-Malays, who were hunters rather than cultivators, remained seminomadic and tribal, whereas the Deutero-Malays settled in scattered riverine or coastal villages on the peninsula and supported themselves primarily through agriculture and fishing.

The Malayan peninsula comprised mostly tropical jungle and was roughly divided along a north-south axis by low mountain spines. Rivers were navigable only for short distances, thus impeding communication. The peninsula was sparsely populated until the mid-nineteenth century, and there was little contact among Malays except for minor trading among neighboring villages. Because land was plentiful and the people few, little value was attached to controlling territory. Prosperity was greatly dependent upon total numbers, which, paradoxically, both moderated the harshness of chiefly rule and encouraged the institution of slavery.

THE INFLUENCE OF THE GREAT CIVILIZATIONS

The Malays in coastal locations had early contact with both Chinese and Indians. The Chinese were interested in ascertaining the military strength of their neighbors, or "barbarians," to the south, in trading, and in exacting tribute, but they were not very interested in attempting to export culture. Consequently, the first culture to have a great impact on the Malays came from India. Contact with seafaring traders from India and influence from the powerful Indianized empires of Java and Sumatra (Indonesia) led to a considerable infusion of Hindu sociopolitical culture into indigenous Malay culture. Sanskrit words and Hindu ritual and regalia, many of which survive to this time, added to the Malay language and blended with local spiritualism (animism). Some of the more important and affluent chiefs, usually those living on port sites, where they could collect tolls and duties, married their daughters to Indian immigrants and adopted much of the Hindu culture. Hindu politics were governed by the notion of a state (*negeri*) that was defined largely in terms of territorial possession, and of a society divided into ruler and subject classifications (with all subjects and land belonging to the ruler). The monarchy required a royal court and elaborate ritual. Many of these rituals survive today: the special vocabulary used in addressing royalty, the reservation of the color yellow for royalty, and the Hindu-derived royal enthronement ceremonies. The control and vague demarcation of territory and the establishment of royal courts, which in turn encouraged the growth of urban settings to support them, gradually transformed the myriad of separate villages into a system of states (although some states were not established until later).

No empires surfaced in Malaysia, probably because it was under the dominance of powerful Indonesian empires, until the rise of Melaka. At the beginning of the fifteenth century, a group of exiled Sumatran Hindus led by Prince Sri Parameswara settled in the small fishing and minor trading village of Melaka. Taking charge, they rapidly transformed the village into a thriving port and transshipment center. They were able to do this because the location was advantageous and the power and influence of Java were then in decline.

ISLAM AND THE MELAKA SULTANATE

Islam, conveyed primarily by Indian traders and missionaries, was beginning to win substantial converts by the fifteenth century. It had become the dominant religion of Aceh (Sumatra), and Melaka had an active and influential Muslim (mostly Tamil Indian) minority. Although there had been an earlier Muslim on the throne, it was not until the 1445 coup against the Hindu Maharaja Sri Parameswara Dewa Shah, who was slain, and the succession of his Muslim half-brother, Sultan Mudzaffar Shah, that Islam became firmly entrenched. Islam was made the official religion of the state, and Melaka became a sultanate. To garner support, the new sultan and his powerful uncle brought some of the leading Malay families into the government, thereby precipitating the process of peaceful conversion of the Malays to Islam. Melaka reached the zenith of its power in the next sixty years and became the primary center for the dissemination of Islam throughout the archipelago.

The Islamic practices that took root in Malaysia were mostly derived from the Indians, who were relatively recent converts themselves. These Islamic practices were derived from the orthodox *Sunni* school, but they were laced with large doses of *Sufi* mysticism, including belief in such things as magical herbs and protective amulets. It is generally believed that the attractions of *Sufism*, which mixed easily with spiritualism, helped account for the rapid and peaceful conversion of *kampung* (village) Malay peasants to Islam (conversely, Hinduism had been a court religion).

Melaka's days of glory came to an abrupt end in 1511, when the Portuguese conquered it. In the sixteenth century, the Portuguese vied with the Dutch for control of the eastern Indonesian island spice trade. They both sought to establish a spice trade monopoly by controlling the sea-lanes, which were supported by fortresses at key points along the route. They were not interested in controlling the hinterlands or the indigenous peoples, except when their fortress colonies were affected by these elements.

The Melaka royal family, members of the government, and many followers fled from Melaka just before it was surrendered to the Portuguese. Some fled to Brunei and others to Johor. Thus the Brunei Sultanate directly profited from the eclipse of Melaka. It established good relations with the Portuguese and prospered economically until the Dutch secured a trade monopoly in the seventeenth century. The Dutch ousted the Portuguese from Melaka in 1641 and destroyed the fortress and port since Melaka rivaled the Dutch port of Batavia (Jakarta); they also diverted trade away from Brunei.

Those who fled to Johor established a new empire at the tip of the peninsula. They exercised control over much of the peninsula but could not dislodge the Portuguese or, later, the Dutch from Melaka, partly because Johor and Aceh could not sink their differences long enough to mount a joint campaign against a common enemy. The Johor royal family recruited Bugis mercenaries from Sulawesi to help fight its enemies. When the fighting died down, however, the Bugis would not return home. Instead, they remained, became involved in court rivalries, and assumed the power behind the Johor throne by the 1720s. They also established their own sultanate in Selangor, attacked Kedah, and supported a rival sultan in Perak.

BRITISH IMPERIAL INTERESTS AND THE ESTABLISHMENT OF COLONIAL RULE

British interests in the region grew as trade between India and China expanded. By the late eighteenth century, the British East India Company was looking for port facilities near the Straits of Melaka for transshipment and also for securing the sea trade lanes, especially against the French. In addition, the British navy was looking for a safe and close harbor for its ships during the monsoon season on the east coast of India. In 1786, a British East India Company agent, Sir Francis Light, acquired the island of Penang for the company through a treaty with the Sultan of Kedah (apparently in return for pledges of support for the sultan against Siamese aggression—support that was never forthcoming from the company). Penang, while beautiful and agreeable, turned out to be less than fully satisfactory. It was not close enough to the Straits of Melaka, and the local timber was not suitable for ship repairs.

In 1819 another company official, Sir Thomas Stamford Raffles, negotiated a treaty with one of the claimants of the Johor throne, who, in return for British recognition of his royal claim and an annual payment, granted the company the right to establish a trading settlement on the island of Singapore (formally ceded to the company in 1824). At the time, Singapore was populated by only about a hundred Malay fishermen and a handful of Chinese agriculturalists, and it was almost completely undeveloped. But, as Raffles himself had concluded, it was ideally situated on the Straits of Melaka, and it had some deep water and sheltered coves that could be made into very good harbors. It was an instant success. Singapore's population grew rapidly (from about 5,000 in 1820 to over 80,000 in 1860), the vast majority of new residents being immigrant Chinese who had heard of the business opportunities, the free port status, and the company's efficient free enterprise and noninterfering administration. Singapore's volume of trade and profits soared, and it quickly replaced Penang as the company's most important outpost for its China trade.

The Dutch protested, however, and claimed that the 1819 treaty was illegal. In 1824, the British and the Dutch concluded a treaty that defined and rationalized their respective spheres of influence. The British gave up their trading settlement in Bencoolen on the west coast of Sumatra (which had been the administrative headquarters for Singapore), and the Dutch gave up Melaka and dropped their protests concerning Singapore. Subsequently, Singapore, Melaka, and Penang were joined administratively to form the Straits Settlements under the company-run government of India.

The interests of the British East India Company were directed primarily to protecting the sea trade lanes and enhancing the profitable China trade (mainly cloth and opium from India in exchange for Chinese silk and tea). The company did not want to incur high administrative or development costs in the Straits Settlements, and it had no interest in expanding into or interfering with the affairs of the peninsula. The Straits merchants, however, were eager to participate in the exploitation of the resources of the peninsula, particularly tin. Although it was company policy not to intervene in the peninsula, and although the company had proclaimed that it would not be drawn in to protect the ill-advised investments of Straits merchants, events conspired to foil this policy.

Tin had been mined in small quantities on the peninsula since the Bronze Age, when it was mixed with copper to make bronze weapons and ornaments. For a short time it was also used as money. Most of the tin was eventually exported to China, where it was used primarily as a decorative substitute for silver. During the sixteenth through nineteenth centuries, first the Portuguese and then the Dutch tried periodically, but unsuccessfully, to enforce a tin monopoly (for European pewter). The mines were owned by the royally connected chiefs, in the Hindu tradition of royal trading, and they conducted all of the business and transactions involved. Because the Malays had little interest in working for wages or for regular hours, especially if employment meant leaving their villages, many of the miners recruited were Chinese.

In the 1850s, large new deposits of tin ore were found in the states of Perak and Selangor. At the same time, demand for tin in the West expanded vastly as a result of the discovery that food could be preserved in tin cans (the use of tin cans by the Union Army during the American Civil War had demonstrated its potential; moreover, as a novelty, canned food had come somewhat into vogue in Europe). The increased demand and promise of riches persuaded the chiefs that they needed to accept large-scale capital investment and technical advice from the Straits merchants in order to expand their operations. More Chinese miners were also required. Chinese indentured laborers from Hong Kong arrived in the Straits

Settlements and then swarmed into the peninsula to work in the mines. This was the beginning of the development of a plural (i.e., ethnically divided) society in Malaysia.

Confusion and chaos soon prevailed in the peninsula. In the frontier setting of the mining towns, newly arrived Chinese were recruited into rival secret societies (generally based on dialects), which then fought each other for possession of the mines and for shares of revenues. The Malay chiefs, many wealthier and more powerful than their rulers, were unable to stem the tide of Chinese immigrants or to enforce order and, in fact, were compelled to take sides in the secret society wars, thus embroiling segments of Malay society in the disturbances. With the monetary stakes so much higher than before, royal succession disputes (largely a product of polygamy and the absence of set rules governing primogeniture) threatened to erupt into widespread civil war. The anarchy jeopardized investments and reduced the volume of trade, and Straits merchants demanded that Britain transfer the Settlements to the Colonial Office (which was done in 1867). Britain was also concerned that the French or Germans might use the disorder as a pretext for intervening in the affairs of the peninsula and thereby establish some political claims to the region.

In fact, when the British sent a new governor, Sir Andrew Clarke, to the Settlements in 1873, they were already alarmed about the destabilization of the Settlements caused by secret society violence (Penang had been at the mercy of rioters for ten days in 1867) and about the possible intervention in the peninsula by the French or Germans. Accordingly, Clarke's rather vague orders were to investigate and report on measures to restore order in the peninsula. Clarke's bold response, which exceeded his orders, led to the establishment of British colonial rule in Malaysia.

The British forward movement in the peninsula began in 1874 when a claimant to the Perak throne, Raja Abdullah, requested Clarke's assistance. Clarke seized the opportunity not only to resolve the succession crisis and the conflict between the secret societies but also to establish a British presence. As a result of the Pangkor Engagement, signed in

January 1874, a commission was established to arbitrate the opposing secret society mine claims, and it was agreed that the Raja Abdullah would be the Sultan of Perak. In addition, the new sultan agreed to accept a British resident whose "advice must be asked and acted upon" in all matters except those concerning Islam and Malay customs. By the late 1880s all of the states, except those in the north under nominal Siamese control, had accepted residents (Johor did not actually have a resident, but it did have a special arrangement with Singapore and a protectorate treaty with Britain).

The residential system was similar to the British "indirect rule" implemented in some parts of Africa. The idea was to exercise political influence by working through the existing political institutions and with the recognized indigenous leaders. By contrast, direct rule involved taking full legal sovereignty of the territory and bypassing or abolishing indigenous institutions (e.g., in direct-ruled Burma, the British abolished the monarchy). Indirect rule was also less costly.

The tasks of the residents in the peninsula included establishing conditions of peace and order, straightening out state finances (most states were quite heavily in debt because few of the moneys collected were given over to state expenses), constructing primary infrastructure (roads and railways), and developing the resources of the state. For the early residents, the assignment was not easy. They had to rely on persuasion since they were not backed by an army, and the carrying out of their rather vague instructions required considerable individual initiative and versatility. The role of the resident and the implications of having a resident were not always fully understood by the rulers, and unhappiness and confusion occasionally resulted. In Perak, Resident J.W.W. Birch was assassinated when his presence became bothersome to the sultan, and the British had to send in troops from Hong Kong and India to arrest the sultan and his co-conspirators (in what has been called the "Perak War"). On the whole, however, the residential system was well accepted because the rulers quickly saw the merits and benefits of it for their states and for themselves; indeed, their financial situation improved and their ceremonial role expanded.

Despite the individual differences exhibited in the implementation of the residential system, a few standard practices did emerge. For example, revenues were now collected by the rulers rather than by the chiefs, who received salaries; systems of taxation were created; and most revenues went into the state treasury rather than into individual pockets. Moreover, state councils comprising the ruler, major chiefs, Chinese leaders, and the resident were established for consultation on state matters.

Over time, the residents ceased being mere advisers and started to assume more executive functions. Occasionally, the rulers and state councils were bypassed, particularly when the residents grew impatient with the ponderous consultations and deliberations required by Malay custom.

In 1909, the present boundaries of Peninsular Malaysia were finally set by the terms of an Anglo-Siamese treaty in which the Siamese surrendered all the claims they had held over the four northern states. These states retained much more independence, having accepted British advisers who functioned strictly *as* advisers.

BRITISH PROTECTORATES IN BORNEO

Brunei, Sarawak, and North Borneo (Sabah) had been in the British orbit for some time, but it was not until 1888 that Britain stepped in formally by establishing protectorates over these three territories.

Brunei had been in a state of slow decline since the sixteenth century. By the late 1830s, the sultanate was politically and economically very weak, and the sultan was unable to exercise any real control over the actions of most of his governors. When a revolt broke out in present-day Sarawak over the harsh rule of the Brunei governor, the sultan's forces were incapable of restoring order. Consequently, at the urging of Singapore merchants, whose trade was being disrupted, the sultan's uncle hired an English adventurer, James Brooke, together with his ship, crew, and naval guns, to put down the revolt in exchange for the governorship. Brooke quickly succeeded, became governor in 1841, and one year later was granted by the sultan a portion of what is now Sarawak in return for tribute. This event inaugurated the rule of the "white rajahs" (namely, the Brooke family), which lasted until 1946. Within four years, the Rajah Brooke had forced the sultan to grant full sovereignty to him, and over the next few decades he annexed piece after piece of Brunei territory to his Sarawak domain.

In the nineteenth century, North Borneo was claimed by both the Sultan of Brunei and the Sultan of Sulu (in the southern Philippines), although neither exercised any real or direct control over the territory. In 1865, the Brunei sultan granted the territory in return for annual payments to an American expatriate adventurer who hoped to colonize the land. Such colonization proved difficult and the grant was sold, eventually ending up in the hands of a partnership of the Dent Brothers—a British company. They negotiated a new treaty for full sovereignty with the Sultan of Brunei in 1877, and in the next year, to play it safe, signed another treaty for virtually the same territory with the Sultan of Sulu. This latter agreement is the source of the Philippine claim to Sabah, which is based on the Filipino contention that a key word in the treaty means to "lease" rather than to "cede." (The Sabah claim is dormant but still unresolved.) In 1881, the Dent Brothers formed a new company (having bought out their partner) and obtained a royal charter to administer the territory. The British North Borneo Chartered Company, which administered North Borneo until 1946, operated under strict regulations, and North Borneo was run more like a colony than a company. It was not a lucrative investment for the shareholders.

In 1888, the British established protectorates over the three countries to stop further annexation of Brunei territory as well as the rivalry developing between the Rajah Brooke and the Chartered Company over the remains of Brunei. (Ironically, major oil fields were discovered in 1929 on the tiny segments of land remaining to Brunei, and Brunei today is the richest country per capita in Southeast Asia.)

THE FEDERATED AND
UNFEDERATED MALAY STATES

Although the residential system functioned effectively in general, the British were beginning to perceive certain short-comings. The residents exercised considerable independence of action, and there was insufficient economic and administrative coordination and cooperation among the states. A new system was introduced to facilitate more control over the residents, to centralize the collection and distribution of revenues in order to help the poorer states, and to provide a modern framework for administrative unity in the peninsula. In 1896, with the consent of the respective rulers, the four states of Perak, Selangor, Pahang, and Negeri Sembilan were combined to form the Federated Malay States (FMS). Within this structure the states surrendered many of their powers, including most of their control of the purse strings, to central authorities in Kuala Lumpur under a resident-general (called a chief secretary from 1911 on).

The four states in the north, which became British protectorates in 1909, along with Johor in the south, became known collectively as the Unfederated Malay States (UMS), although they were formally linked neither to one another nor to the FMS. In the 1920s and 1930s, Britain made some attempts to entice them to agree to more unity and central-ization (under the cloak of "decentralization" and with various incentives), but the rulers of the UMS resisted all moves that threatened their state powers.

IMMIGRATION AND "PROTECTION"
OF THE MALAYS UNDER THE BRITISH

When colonial rule was extended to the peninsula, the British continued to encourage the immigration of Chinese to work the west coast tin mines and to provide economic support systems in the urban centers growing up around the prosperous mines and ports. With economic expansion, the numbers of immigrants multiplied, and soon the Chinese were owner-operating some of the mines and running most family-sized urban businesses, from retail trading to manufacturing and import-export firms.

In 1877, rubber seedlings, reportedly wild seeds taken surreptitiously from Brazil, were sent to the Botanic Gardens in Singapore. The rubber trees thrived, and after the turn of the century, when Henry Ford discovered a means of mass producing automobiles, the demand for rubber for tires soared. Thousands of acres in the peninsula were planted as rubber tree plantations, which were managed for the most part by expatriate Britons from Ceylon (Sri Lanka). Neither the Malays nor the Chinese were willing to live and work on the isolated rubber plantations, so the European planters arranged for the immigration of indentured workers from India, thus completing Malaysia's ethnic picture. Like the Chinese, the Indians also spread out into other occupations, most notably into the retail trades and the railways.

The British considered these overseas immigrants to be "birds of passage" (or, in the modern lexicon, "guest workers"), who would return to their home countries after making good money. Consequently, the British made no effort to integrate the races. In fact, the immigrant communities were encouraged to oversee their own affairs and to finance and run their own vernacular schools, newspapers, and associations. Many of these immigrants did in fact return home, but a large and ever-increasing number stayed and set down roots. By the time the British finally listened to the pleadings of the Malay elite to impose immigration quotas (i.e., in 1928 in the Straits Settlements, and in 1930 in the FMS), there were as many non-Malays concentrated in the urban areas of the west coast and the Straits Settlements as Malays in the peninsula.

British policy, well meaning but destructively paternalistic, was to "protect" the Malays, the favored indigenous race, from economic competition, ugly commercialism, and the deleterious effects that modern urban life was considered to pose for their culture. The Malay peasants were encouraged to maintain their traditional way of life by means of restrictions on the sale of Malay land, various incentives, and the limiting of Malay education to basic primary subjects designed not to make traditional life less acceptable. The Malay aristocracy approved of this policy, because it helped preserve the basically feudal royal establishment and maintain Malay deference to rank. The scions of the aristocracy attended the best schools in England and/or (after 1905) the elite Malay College at Kuala Kangsar, and entered the elite branches of the civil service.

Because deference was such an important factor in Malay culture, and because the aristocracy supported British rule, early Malay nationalism (itself a pan-Islamic intellectual variant) stood no chance of gaining a mass following. British "protection" of the Malays spared their culture from the convulsions of rapid change, but it simultaneously condemned the Malays to being the most undereducated and economically unadvanced of the races at the time of independence.

THE DIVIDE: WORLD WAR II

Between December 1941 and August 1945, the Malayan peninsula was occupied by the Japanese. The main effect of the occupation, aside from economic decay and the destruction of the "myth of white supremacy," was the worsening of ethnic relations. The Japanese largely succeeded in wooing Malays of all classes to accept or acquiesce to their "Asia for the Asians" war effort. Few Malays seemed aware of the contradictions between Japan's anticolonialist rhetoric and the aims of its Greater East Asia Co-Prosperity Sphere, which was to make Southeast Asia the supplier of raw materials to feed Japanese industry and the buyer of Japanese finished products, as well as a colonizing location for excess Japanese population. While the collaboration of the Malays was sought, the Japanese considered all Chinese to be enemies—an historical legacy exacerbated by Japanese frustrations with the conduct of the war in China. Indians were made to choose between supporting the radical independence movement of Subhas Chandra Bose or facing the consequences of being regarded as pro-British. One result was that the guerrilla Malayan People's Anti-Japanese Army (MPAJA), the precursor of the Malayan Communist party (MCP), was almost entirely

Chinese, and the police forces responsible for harassing them were almost entirely Malay.

The war ended before an Allied invasion of the peninsula could be mounted, and for several weeks there was no government. Anarchy reigned and widespread ethnic "score-settling" ensued, thereby greatly increasing ethnic fears and hostilities.

THE MALAYAN UNION
AND POSTWAR NATIONALISM

Before the war had ended, the British had decided to introduce a new political scheme in the peninsula when civilian colonial rule was resumed. The Malayan Union, as the scheme was called, would unite the FMS, UMS, Penang, and Melaka as a single crown colony (Singapore, because of its large Chinese population and its strategic value, would become a separate crown colony). The long-term aim of the Union was constitutional progress toward eventual self-government. With this scheme, the peninsula would be unified under a centralized government, the special position of the Malays would be canceled, and the rulers would be reduced to figureheads. Furthermore, liberal citizenship regulations would encourage the integration of the non-Malays into the polity. This move followed from the recognition that most of the non-Malays were not "birds of passage"; it was also a measure of appreciation for the role played by the non-Malays in resisting the Japanese war effort.

The Malayan Union was promulgated in April 1946 after the rulers, some threatened with dismissal for wartime collaboration, hastily signed over their sovereignty to the British (in the MacMichael Treaties). The Union represented a radical departure from prewar British policy, and the Malays were instantly alarmed, visualizing similarities between their situation and that of the Red Indians of North America, with their culture consigned to the back room of a museum.

The Malayan Union provided the impetus for the birth of Malay nationalism. Unlike prewar nationalist groups, this movement joined together Malays of all states and social classes and was led by the aristocracy. In May 1946, the United Malays National Organization (UMNO) was formed under the leadership of Dato Onn bin Jaafar (who came from an aristocratic Johor family) to oppose the Union and secure the survival of the Malay race. Mass Malay demonstrations, boycotts, and protests showed the shocked British the extent and depth of Malay outrage, and UMNO proposals for a federal scheme offered an alternative to consider.

Fearful of open Malay rebellion, already facing an internal security challenge posed by primarily non-Malay Communist-led labor union strife and violence, and with the majority of the non-Malays showing little enthusiasm for the Union, the British announced in July 1946 that the Malayan Union would be replaced by a federal scheme, the details of which would be worked out by UMNO, the rulers, and the British. There was no provision for the representation of the non-Malays at the constitutional talks.

THE FEDERATION OF MALAYA

In February 1948, the Federation of Malaya came into being. It was a federation of the same states as those in the Union, and the central government reserved for itself most important powers. But there was a list of state powers, many of the functions of the rulers were reinstituted, and Malay "special rights" were restored. Most important, strict citizenship provisions, seen as the key protection for the survival of the Malay race, were instituted. UMNO's victory in securing the federation agreement solidified Malay nationalism and channeled it behind an organization led by the Malay aristocracy. From that point until now, UMNO has been the dominant political force in the country.

Although the non-Malays had had the most to gain by the Malayan Union, they were slow to react to the forces seeking its demise. Chinese and Indian nationalism, which was internally fragmented, had been directed almost exclusively to events transpiring in China and India, respectively. It was not until the federation scheme had become a *fait accompli*, bringing with it a demonstration of UMNO-led

Malay power, that Chinese and Indian nationalism became Malaya-centered. The Malayan Chinese Association (MCA), formed in 1949, and the Malayan Indian Congress (MIC), formed in 1946, turned their attention toward protecting and promoting the rights of their respective ethnic communities.

THE "EMERGENCY"

For nearly two years, the Malayan Communist party tested British resolve and internal security capabilities by radicalizing the trade union movement and resorting to violence. In response, the British passed tough and restrictive labor laws that undermined the ability of the MCP to operate successfully through front organizations. Beginning in mid-1948, members of the MCP, almost entirely Chinese, returned to the jungles and began a guerrilla war of national liberation. At the peak of this activity, the number of armed rebels was over 9,000. In addition to the labor laws and the frustration of the non-Malays over the federation agreement, the decision to resort to insurgency probably had something to do with the resolutions passed at the famous Calcutta meeting of young Communists in February 1948, given that revolts had broken out simultaneously throughout Southeast Asia. The British declared a nationwide state of emergency that lasted until 1960 (and, in fact, several hundred guerrillas are still operating in the jungle areas along the Thai border). The "Emergency" directly resulted in about 11,000 deaths.

The MCP never came close to fomenting a national struggle or threatening to seize power. Because it was almost entirely Chinese and could not attract Malays or Indians to its cause, the MCP could not successfully claim the banner of anticolonialism and nationalism. Moreover, the British counterinsurgency strategy, especially the Briggs Plan, proved highly successful. Through the Briggs Plan more than 500,000 Chinese were relocated in barbed-wire and guarded "New Villages," where they could not be threatened by or tempted into assisting the guerrillas. As might have been expected, however, this relocation caused some hardship and bitterness toward the government, despite considerable MCA work in providing financial and social assistance. The New Villages in general remain antigovernment in their voting behavior.

FIRST ELECTIONS AND FORMATION
OF THE ALLIANCE PARTY

Although the eventual granting of independence was in line with British policy, the British had also let it be known that they would not turn the country over to one ethnic group alone; adequate protection for all groups was necessary, and the various communities needed to demonstrate that they could cooperate politically and live in peace.

With this in mind, some early attempts at ethnic cooperation were made. In 1949, a Communities Liaison Committee (CLC) was formed, comprising the top leaders of the ethnic communities and a British official. The recommendations of the CLC carried no official clout, and the committee itself was criticized by many if not most Malays. However, the CLC was able to establish some principles—in particular, the rejection of communal electoral rolls and the acceptance of the moral obligation that the non-Malays should help improve the economic position of the Malays.

In 1951, UMNO President Dato Onn attempted to get the UMNO rank-and-file to open its membership to all ethnic groups. When this was flatly rejected, Dato Onn threatened to resign. Although the ploy had previously been successful, this time he was allowed to do so. He was succeeded as president by Tunku Abdul Rahman, nephew of the Sultan of Kedah and former Cambridge University student with a reputation as a playboy. Dato Onn started a multiethnic party, the Independence of Malaya party (IMP), which was inaugurated with great ceremony, high expectations, and British hopes that it would provide the answer to ethnic cooperation. Problems soon arose, however. The Tunku warned that the IMP would undermine Malay interests and threatened to expel any UMNO member who joined. Except for personal friends of Dato Onn, Malays did not join the IMP; as a result, its multiethnic credibility was greatly diminished. The Chinese were also cautious and hung back, while the Indians were

The "Father of Independence," Tunku Abdul Rahman, in Melaka in 1956. He is waving a 100-year-old *keris,* a traditional Malay knife, presented to him upon his return from London following talks on independence—the Merdeka Mission. (Courtesy of Datuk Rais Yatim and the Malaysian Ministry of Information.)

interested but sought association for the MIC as a whole
rather than individual memberships.

Municipal elections for several urban areas were scheduled for 1951–1952. The key election occurred in Kuala Lumpur
in February 1952. The participants included UMNO, MCA,
IMP, the Labour party, and some independents. At the beginning of the campaign, UMNO, which had financial problems, surprisingly formed an ad hoc alliance with the MCA,
which had money but was lacking enfranchised Chinese, to
oppose the threat both parties felt was emanating from the
brand of noncommunalism proposed by the IMP. The two
parties agreed not to oppose each other; the MCA, which
financed the campaign, was given some seats to contest,
whereas UMNO instructed its followers to vote for the MCA
candidates. There was no attempt at policy coordination or
agreement. The partnership worked extraordinarily well, with
UMNO-MCA winning 9 of the 12 seats. The IMP, the pre-
election favorite, suffered a devastating defeat (in winning
only two seats), from which it never recovered. The party
was quietly deregistered in 1954, ending the first and only
genuine chance for a successful multiethnic party.

The national leaders of UMNO and the MCA allowed
similar temporary alliances in the ensuing municipal elections,
and the arrangement proved equally successful. In 1953, a
permanent and national Alliance Organization (changed to
the Alliance party in 1957) was established. One year later,
the MIC, which had been floundering in the political wilderness, voted to join the coalition. The Alliance thus consisted
of three parties representing the major ethnic groups in
Malaya. From the beginning UMNO viewed itself, and was
seen, as the major party of the coalition—the first among
equals (the Malays were the largest ethnic group, they were
the indigenous race, and the electorate was then about 87
percent Malay).

The Alliance formula still had its skeptics, however, and
the major test was Malaya's first national elections for Legislative Council seats in 1955. It was recognized that the party
forming the government at this election would likely lead the
country to independence. The thorny problem of the division

of seats was resolved by the party elites, and the Alliance campaigned on the goal of early independence, which they claimed would be hastened by the Alliance's demonstration of ethnic cooperation. They avoided all unresolved contentious ethnic issues. The results gave the Alliance a dominating 51 of the 52 seats.

THE "BARGAIN" AND INDEPENDENCE

The British now accepted the fact that a multiethnic party was not viable and that the Alliance represented the best possible formula for ethnic harmony. All that stood in the way of independence was a constitution that would satisfy the British that the rights and privileges of all of the communities were safeguarded. In other words, the Alliance leaders could no longer avoid vexing ethnic issues.

With independence as the "carrot" being dangled, the top leaders of UMNO, MCA, and MIC sat down in private and, over a grinding four-month period of intense negotiations, worked out a *quid pro quo* package deal that has become known as the "Bargain." The essence of the Bargain was the acceptance by the non-Malay leaders that the Malays, as the indigenous race, were entitled to political dominance, while in return the Malay leaders recognized that the socioeconomic pursuits of the non-Malays should not be infringed upon. Most of the Bargain was incorporated into the independence constitution. Islam would be the state religion (but freedom of religion would be guaranteed), the powers and prerogatives of the rulers would be maintained, and Malay land reservations would be continued. In addition, Malay "special rights" would be upheld and protected under Article 153, which could not be amended except with the consent of the Conference of Rulers (see Chapter 5)—rights such as reservations or quotas for Malays in the federal public service and armed forces, for business permits or licences, and for educational scholarships (later amended to include university admissions). Finally, Malay would become the sole official language in ten years' time (beginning in 1967), unless Parliament decided otherwise. For the non-Malays, the constitution would incorporate the principle of *jus soli* (the right of citizenship by virtue of birth in a country), and naturalization regulations would be liberalized. Beyond all other considerations, this last measure was what the non-Malays wanted. It was also the demand that the Malays found most wrenching to accept, inasmuch as they were worried about "numbers" and viewed restricted citizenship as their chief protection.

Having agreed to the Bargain, the Alliance elites then had to convince their respective ethnic communities that, although no community could get everything it wanted, the compromises provided a workable solution that would enable the country to gain its independence. Segments of each community rejected the terms, but the majority appeared to accept the Bargain and progress toward independence continued.

As agreed to by the Alliance elites, the rulers, and the British government, and in addition to the constitutional provisions of the Bargain, the independence constitution called for a federal system of parliamentary government headed by a constitutional monarch (*yang dipertuan agung*) who, uniquely, would be elected for a five-year term by the rulers from among themselves at a meeting of the Conference of Rulers. Parliament would be the supreme law-making body, although it could not pass laws on matters reserved for the states (such as Muslim law, land, agriculture and forestry, mining, and local government). Parliament would consist of a more powerful elected House of Representatives (Dewan Rakyat) and a less powerful Senate (Dewan Negara), the latter of which would have some power to delay bills. Nearly all constitutional amendments would require the votes of at least two-thirds of the total membership of both houses of Parliament. All bills would be presented to the *agung* for his assent before becoming law. It was understood that the assent of the *agung*, as a constitutional monarch, would be automatically forthcoming, since he would act in accordance with the advice of the cabinet. As will be described in the next chapter, however, this constitutional assumption led to a crisis in 1983. Elections would be held at least every five years, and the majority party would form the government. The leader of the majority party would become the prime minister, who in turn would name members of his cabinet to act as the executive authority of the country.

The constitution also provided for an independent judiciary entrusted to pronounce on the legality and validity of laws passed by Parliament and to interpret the meaning of any provision of the constitution. Finally, through Article 150, the constitution granted power to the *agung*, acting on cabinet advice, to declare a state of emergency if national security was threatened. The emergency powers were extensive, including the suspension of parliamentary rule.

With the constitutional details worked out to the satisfaction of the concerned parties, the Federation of Malaya became an independent country and a member of the British Commonwealth under a multiethnic Alliance government headed by Prime Minister Tunku Abdul Rahman in a peaceful transfer of power on August 31, 1957.

3

History Since Independence

Two years after independence, the Alliance government could take pride in its economic accomplishments, the ethnic peace that prevailed, and the nation's strong counterinsurgency performance. Yet, the Alliance did face a few problems as the campaign for the 1959 federal election began. The massive attraction held by the goal of independence was no longer available to cement over divisive forces. Furthermore, with the implementation of various aspects of the Bargain, some ethnic disenchantment was being voiced. Finally, with the advent of liberalized citizenship regulations, many more non-Malays were enfranchised (the Chinese now constituted about 36 percent of the electorate and the Indians about 7 percent).

In the state elections that preceded the federal one, the Pan-Malayan Islamic Party—now called "Partai Islam Se-Malaysia" and known by its Malay-Arabic acronym, PAS—won majority control of the two northern and heavily Malay-populated states of Kelantan and Terengganu. PAS had campaigned on Malay nationalist themes and invoked the appeal of Islam. It had accused UMNO of "selling out" the birthrights of the Malays through its compromises with infidels. As "proof" that the Chinese were really running the country, PAS officials showed rural Malay peasants the new dollar bills, each signed by a Chinese individual—namely, Henry Lee, the minister of finance.

The success of this "outbidding" by PAS worried UMNO elites, and consequently they were in no mood for conciliation

31

when the 1959 "July crisis" with the MCA broke out. By mid-1958, the MCA had split into two camps: the moderate leaders who had negotiated the Bargain and brought the MCA into the Alliance, and the "new bloods" (or Chinese firsters), who demanded more equality in the Alliance, more electoral seats for the MCA, more policy concessions concerning language and education, and also the initiation of talks aimed at a merger with Singapore. The old leaders, represented by its first president, Tun Tan Cheng Lock, were ousted in MCA party elections, and the "new bloods" gained control. When the new leaders' demands became public in July 1959, the Tunku issued an ultimatum threatening to break up the Alliance. The MCA central committee eventually capitulated to the Tunku's demands, but many "new bloods" either voluntarily exited from the party or were expelled and stood in the election as independents.

Any lingering misconceptions concerning the identity of the dominant partner of the coalition were permanently resolved by the crisis. However, the timing of the crisis, coming as it did just before the election (the Alliance election manifesto was published just one week before polling, having been delayed by the crisis), weakened the Alliance's performance. It won 74 of 104 seats, but its popular vote declined sharply to just over 51 percent. The fractured MCA fared the worst of the partners (winning only 19 of 31 seats), with most of its losses occurring in the heavily Chinese-populated urban areas and New Villages. This was the beginning of the MCA dilemma: Its safest seats were those in Malay-majority constituencies; it could not win in areas heavily populated by its own ethnic members. The biggest gains among the opposition parties went to PAS (13 seats); the Socialist Front, or SF—a coalition between a Malay and a non-Malay party based on ideology (8 seats); and the Perak-based non-Malay People's Progressive party, or PPP (4 seats).

THE MALAYSIA PROPOSAL

The idea of uniting Singapore with the peninsula had been debated for several years, but the Federation's Malay elites, mindful of Singapore's large Chinese population, had shown little interest in the idea. Consequently, it was quite a surprise to many when in May 1961 the Tunku proposed the creation of Malaysia by linking Singapore and the Borneo states (Sarawak, North Borneo, and Brunei) with the Federation of Malaya.

Two factors accounted for the Tunku's change of heart. First, the British had made it known that they were interested in relinquishing their costly responsibilities in Borneo. In this way, they provided an opportunity for rekindling the idea of a merger with Singapore, as the indigenous (and partly Muslim) population of the Borneo states would offset the inclusion of Singapore's Chinese population. Actually, the Malay elites in Kuala Lumpur only poorly understood the ethnic composition of Sarawak and North Borneo (renamed Sabah in 1963). They knew correctly that Brunei's population was predominantly Malay-Muslim. They realized that there were some Malays in Sarawak and some other indigenous Muslims in both Sarawak and Sabah. They tended, however, to consider all indigenous peoples to be sympathetic to Malay efforts and goals and, hence, to be an effective counterpoise to Singapore's Chinese population. This was not entirely to be the case. At various times some of the major indigenous groups, particularly the non-Muslim ones, have resisted suggestions and directions emanating from Kuala Lumpur.

Second, by 1961 the ruling party of Singapore, the People's Action party (PAP) under Lee Kuan Yew, had split and was in trouble. The pro-Communist faction had formed a new party (the Barisan Sosialis), which was threatening to wrest power from the PAP through the electoral process. With MCP guerrillas still operating in the northern jungles of the peninsula, the Tunku was distressed at the prospect of a "Cuba" on his southern flank. With Singapore inside the proposed federation and subject to Kuala Lumpur's stringent internal security regulations, the Communists could be prevented from coming to power. Further, the merger idea was popular in Singapore and, once proposed, gave an electoral edge to the PAP against its pro-Communist challenger.

Singapore and the British responded quickly and favorably to Kuala Lumpur's Malaysia proposal, and early agreements in principle were easily reached. In Borneo, however, there was some hesitation and confusion—and even some alarm.

SARAWAK AND NORTH BORNEO (SABAH)

In 1946, when neither the Rajah Brooke nor the British North Borneo Chartered Company possessed sufficient capital for postwar reconstruction, Sarawak and North Borneo were transferred to the British as directly ruled crown colonies (Brunei remained a protectorate). The change from company to colony was easily accepted in North Borneo and required only minor administrative adjustments. It also offered the possibility of new capital for development purposes. However, the "cession" of Sarawak from the Rajah Brooke to the British was opposed by some groups—notably, a segment of the Malays who had been favored for government positions under Brooke rule, as well as some Ibans who believed that the Brookes had protected their traditions and given the Ibans high prestige. The cession split the Malay community and to some extent exacerbated Iban geographic divisions. The unfortunate first British governor of Sarawak was assassinated only days after his arrival. Resistance to British rule subsided quickly, but the intraethnic rifts continued and later complicated the Sarawak political scene.

At the time of the Tunku's Malaysia proposal in May 1961, the Borneo states were socially, economically, and politically underdeveloped. Literacy rates were low, health facilities were poor, the economies were dependent upon primary product exports, and agricultural practices still widely featured shifting cultivation. Moreover, communications were poor, with few roads, limited air service (most travel was by boat), few telephones and radios, and only small newspaper circulations (mostly English or Chinese language papers). Except in the larger towns, there was little or no electricity. In addition, only the most rudimentary political development had occurred. Sarawak had its first local elections in 1959 and Sabah in December 1962. Only one political party existed at the time of the Tunku's proposal—the Chinese-dominated Sarawak United People's party (SUPP).

Initially, there were considerable reservations in the Borneo states over the Malaysia proposal. Many Chinese preferred the security and economic freedom of action provided by the British and were not anxious to come under Malay domination, as had their brethren in Malaya. Moreover, a number of indigenous non-Muslim groups, and even some Muslims, retained (through folklore) memories of repression by the Brunei Malays and were reluctant to become part of a Malay-dominated polity unless they were provided with ironclad safeguards. In addition, some Borneo leaders entertained hopes that a federation consisting of just the Borneo states could be established.

The Malaysia proposal set in motion a period of rapid and intense political development. A myriad of political parties sprang into existence, all based primarily on ethnicity. Coalitions were also attempted. Some of these parties opposed Malaysia, and an early fact-finding team, the Cobbold Commission, recorded these reservations in 1962. However, after intensive wooing and lobbying by Kuala Lumpur, as well as promises of safeguards and special states rights, most shifted to support the proposal. As late as October 1962, three parties (one of them a Brunei party) still opposed Malaysia. However, a United Nations Malaysia Mission team analyzed local election results, accepted submissions on behalf of various groups, and decided that there was a majority approval for the scheme.

THE FORMATION OF MALAYSIA

In July 1963, as progress toward the creation of Malaysia quickened, the Sultan of Brunei withdrew from the London talks and declared that Brunei would not join the Federation of Malaysia. Apparently, differences between the sultan and Kuala Lumpur over the sharing of oil revenues, over the sultan's status vis-à-vis the peninsular rulers, and over his eligibility to become *agung* could not be resolved, among other reasons.

The official date for the formation of Malaysia was postponed from August 31 (which, nevertheless, is celebrated now as Malaysia Day) to September 16, 1963, to allow the UN team to ascertain the views of the Borneo people. The UN report was favorable. Because of a crucial election in Singapore, however, the Tunku felt compelled to announce the date for the creation of Malaysia prior to the completion of the UN report. The sense of urgency in speedily proclaiming the formation of Malaysia before all details were completed and before international relations had been taken through all of the diplomatic hoops brought Kuala Lumpur into deeper conflict with the Philippines and Indonesia (see Chapter 7).

The Constitution of Malaysia

The new constitution was a more complex version of the 1957 independence constitution for Malaya. As a safeguard, Sarawak and Sabah were allowed certain state powers denied the peninsular states, such as control of immigration, additional sources of revenue, and special concessions concerning language and religion. Furthermore, indigenous persons were added to the "special rights" category for Malays under Article 153. In addition, the Borneo states were given a disproportionately high number of parliamentary seats, and special provisions were listed for financial grants. On the whole, Kuala Lumpur's relationship with the Borneo states, and with Singapore, was much more genuinely federal than was the case with the peninsular states.

Singapore's constitutional position contained some of the same safeguards as well as certain additional powers governing education and labor. To balance these concessions, however, Singapore was given fewer parliamentary seats than its numbers warranted and its people remained "Singapore citizens"—on a par with "federal citizens" but distinct (and thus unable to participate politically elsewhere in the Federation).

Economic details and disputes concerning income tax revenues, common market arrangements, and so on were not fully resolved before the formation of Malaysia and soon became a major source of friction and rancor between Kuala Lumpur and Singapore.

The 1964 General Elections

The general elections of 1964 (held for Peninsular Malaysia only) were conducted against the backdrop of Indonesia's aggressive *Konfrontasi* ("Confrontation") campaign against Malaysia (see Chapter 7) and growing tensions between Kuala Lumpur and Singapore. Although the Alliance campaigned on its economic development achievements and continuing ethnic peace, its strongest issue was *Konfrontasi*. In this connection, the Alliance could equate solid electoral support for the government with patriotism. Members of the opposition, some of whom had initially opposed the creation of Malaysia, were disadvantaged. Most echoed agreement with the government in opposing Indonesian aggression while rather lamely presenting some social and economic criticisms. The party that had been most adamantly opposed to Malaysia and that remained somewhat unreconciled to it was PAS. It had taken a pro-Indonesian stance, which it viewed as pro-Islamic pan-Indonesianism. Some PAS members were in detention as a result of their activities, and to many the party seemed compromised. Still, in some of the rural Malay-populated areas, PAS could justify its position in terms of promoting Islam.

One of the surprises of the election was the decision by Singapore's Lee Kuan Yew to spread the PAP's influence by having the party contest some peninsular seats in MCA constituencies. The PAP's justification was that the MCA was a weak and effete party run by big Chinese *towkays* (businessmen), whose candidates could not defeat the Socialist Front's Chinese candidates. However, the Tunku believed that Lee had promised that the PAP would not participate and felt that he had been "stabbed in the back." The PAP challenge did not amount to much, but it severely damaged Kuala Lumpur–Singapore relations. To the Tunku, loyalty and honesty were two of the highest virtues. After the PAP's participation in the election, the personal rift between Lee and himself could never be repaired.

The election results gave the Alliance an increased majority in Parliament. It won 89 of 104 seats, with just over

58 percent of the popular vote. In the opposition, PAS won 9 seats, SF won 2, PPP won 2, PAP won 1, and the United Democratic party (a Penang-based primarily Chinese party) won 1. In the state elections, the Alliance retained control of ten states but failed to recapture Kelantan from PAS, despite *Konfrontasi* and promises of large development funds.

Singapore's Expulsion from Malaysia

One consequence of the rapidity with which Malaysia had been formed was that important areas of economic and social coordination and agreement between Kuala Lumpur and Singapore were still awaiting resolution in 1964 and 1965. More devastating still were the political ambiguities that clouded perceptions of Singapore's proper role in the Federation. Kuala Lumpur regarded Singapore as a rich Chinese state (the "New York" of Malaysia) that had been given certain extra powers and privileges but was just a state nonetheless. The federal government sought to limit and contain Singapore's influence to the island itself. Singapore, however, viewed itself as more powerful and important than the other states (after all, Lee Kuan Yew's accepted title was "prime minister," not the regular state designation of "chief minister"), and it sought to expand its influence nationally.

After the PAP's unexpected participation in the 1964 peninsular elections, relations between Kuala Lumpur and Singapore plummeted. Exacerbating the tension and rancor between the two was the fact that the political styles of the Alliance and the PAP were polar opposites. The Alliance elites privately worked out policies involving ethnic accommodation and then presented a calm and united public front. When policies were given a public hearing, they were presented as a fait accompli. Issues to which no agreement could be found were quietly "swept under the carpet." The PAP, on the other hand, tended to take issues still under debate directly to the public forum, oblivious to the fact that in an ethnically divided society, the incitement of ethnic emotions can be dangerous.

From the time of the 1964 elections, Lee and the PAP took the offensive. First, the PAP sought to replace the MCA in the Alliance. Turned down flatly by the Tunku, the PAP then sought a coalition with the Alliance. Rebuked again, Lee began attacking the Alliance and challenging the terms of the Bargain. He denied that the Malays were more indigenous than other groups and therefore entitled to any special claims to political predominance. Further, while alleging (after some ethnic arithmetic) that the non-Malays actually outnumbered the Malays, he called for a "Malaysian Malaysia" with full political equality.

Lee's actions had the effect of stirring up the ethnic anxieties and fears of the Malays. Malay "ultras" demanded Lee's arrest, a federal takeover of Singapore, and various other demonstrations of Malay power. Young Chinese were also charged up by Lee's rhetoric and became eager for a new political formula. "Chinese chauvinists" called for an end to the Bargain and the Alliance system. Ethnic outbidders undermined the ability of Alliance moderates to convince their ethnic constituencies to accept compromises, and ugly race riots broke out in Singapore in the summer and early fall of 1964.

Still determined to force a realignment, the PAP in 1965 began putting together a united opposition front (the Malaysian Solidarity Convention), composed of five opposition parties, in order to oppose the Alliance. However, in June 1965 the Tunku, while convalescing in a London clinic with a painful bout of shingles, became convinced that if widespread ethnic conflict was to be avoided, Singapore had to be separated out of the Federation. Talks on the terms of separation (the frantic PAP leaders sought a less drastic alternative) were conducted during July. On August 9, 1965, the Tunku announced Singapore's separation from Malaysia.

The 1969 General Elections and the May 13th Riots

Although Singapore had been cut away from the Federation with surgical precision, the ideas and issues raised and the ethnic militancy aroused remained potent. In the peninsula, a new political party, the Democratic Action party (DAP), a direct successor to the PAP, was allowed to register and carry on the campaign for a "Malaysian Malaysia." In Sarawak and Sabah, issues and grievances regarding states' rights were taken up again.

The whole tone of politics between 1964 and 1969 was characterized by growing ethnic extremism. The date for making Malay the sole official language in 1967 was yet another occasion for shrill ethnic demands. The Tunku made some compromises in the 1967 Language Act that allowed for the continued use of English for some official purposes, but the Chinese chauvinists, who had been demanding that Chinese be made an official language alongside Malay, were not mollified. Supported by the DAP, they quickly demanded the establishment of a privately funded Chinese-language Merdeka University. When this was refused by the government, it became an emotional cause célèbre in the Chinese community. Similarly, large segments of the Malay community, including university students, PAS, and some influential members of UMNO, strenuously objected to any language compromises and felt that the Malays had been betrayed by the concessions.

Although the language bill was passed into law without violence, militant forces were in fact gaining momentum. The Tunku's efforts to be what Karl von Vorys described as a "super-communal arbiter,"[1] his moderation (from the Malay perspective) in dealing with Singapore, and his compromises on the official language issue had the negative effect of undermining his authority and legitimacy as the chief spokesman for the Malays. The MCA and MIC leaders were also caught in a bind: They were unable to support the most ardent non-Malay demands and thus appeared powerless to defend non-Malay interests.

Opposition "outbidding" was rampant during the campaign for the 1969 elections, which was also the longest campaign period ever, and the two election-related deaths (a rarity in Malaysia) that occurred led to emotional public funerals. Increasingly, Alliance candidates privately broke away from national policy positions and invoked ethnic appeals.

The peninsular results gave the Alliance 66 of 103 parliamentary seats and just over 48 percent of the popular vote. As yet, there were no returns from Sarawak or Sabah because of the staggered voting there. In the peninsular state elections, the Alliance failed again to win Kelantan, lost Penang, and did not have clear majorities in the two key Malay states of Perak and Selangor, thus prompting rumors that a non-Malay might become *menteri besar* (the chief political figure in the state). The results stunned the Alliance, although it still retained federal power, and the MCA, which had won only 13 of 33 seats, announced that since it had been rejected by the Chinese community it would not accept any cabinet posts.

On May 12, 1969, a police permit was given for a "victory celebration" parade in Kuala Lumpur that had been organized by two primarily Chinese opposition parties. It was a huge and emotional demonstration rather than a parade, and Chinese and Malays exchanged angry racial taunts in the streets as the procession moved along. The following day, May 13, the police inexplicably issued a permit for a Malay counterdemonstration. All morning, truckloads of Malays armed with *parangs* (long knives) arrived in the city. The counterdemonstration quickly degenerated into an uncontrolled battleground of racial violence, mindless murder, and widespread arson.

A proclamation of a nationwide state of emergency was quickly issued, and federal troops moved into Kuala Lumpur to restore order. The elections in Sarawak and Sabah were suspended, a strict curfew was imposed to prevent the violence from spreading, and a new sedition ordinance banned all political activity. Under the proclamation, Parliament was suspended and extensive governing powers were given to a National Operations Council (NOC) under the directorship of Deputy Prime Minister Tun Razak. In theory, the NOC ruled jointly with the cabinet under the Tunku's direction; in practice almost all real power was exercised by the NOC.

A NEW FORMULA FOR POLITICAL RULE

The May 13th riots proved to be a watershed. Subsequently, the Bargain was discarded and the Alliance party

became irrelevant. Malay political hegemony was proclaimed
as a political fact of life to avoid any future misunderstandings.
The new formula retained features of elite accommodation,
such as the formation of a broad coalition, the principle of
consultation and compromise, and the practice of multiethnic
representation in the cabinet. But the "new realism" meant
that key issues considered vital to Malay interests were non-
negotiable. Furthermore, "politicking" was proclaimed to be
dangerous and wasteful of national energies, and laws were
passed to restrict political debate and to limit the political
actions of ethnic outbidders.

After order had been restored and NOC rule was func-
tioning effectively, Tun Razak met with some of his closest
Malay political associates to determine the causes of the riots
as well as a course of action for the future. They decided
that the root cause of the riots was Malay economic grievances,
and this led to the formulation of the New Economic Policy
(NEP) in 1970 (see Chapter 6).

Politically, Tun Razak and his associates considered a
number of options, such as indefinitely continuing NOC rule
(urged by many Malays), rule by an all-Malay government
(favored by PAS and other "ultras"), single-party rule, and
a return to the *status quo ante*. In the end, they decided to
return to a form of parliamentary rule and to adopt a grand
coalition strategy coupled with restrictions limiting political
competition. They believed that the Westminster model of
democracy ignored the sociopolitical realities of Malaysia and
concluded that the basic problem with the Alliance was its
style of ambiguity and its tendency to put off making difficult
decisions. In its stead, they wanted a broad-based government
led by the Malays and stating firm and clear political goals
and policies.

In January 1970, Tun Razak set up the National Con-
sultative Council (NCC) to determine "positive and practical
guidelines for interracial cooperation." Invitations to participate were sent to all major political parties and numerous
functional, religious, and regional groups. Only the DAP and
Partai Rakyat declined to participate. The discussions of the
NCC were confidential (no minutes were kept), and decisions

required a consensus rather than simple majority rule. The NCC was able to agree on the NEP, a national ideology (*rukunegara*), and certain constitutional amendments. The deliberations apparently convinced Tun Razak that NOC rule could be terminated.

Parliamentary rule was reinstituted in February 1971 under Tun Razak, who had become prime minister in September 1970 when the Tunku retired. The first business before Parliament in 1971 was to pass the Constitution (Amendment) Bill, which it promptly did. This act "entrenched" certain ethnically sensitive provisions of the constitution (e.g., citizenship, language, Malay special rights) by making any amendments to these articles subject to the approval of the Conference of Rulers. In addition, the Sedition Act was amended to prohibit the "questioning" of sensitive issues, even within Parliament and the state assemblies.

The Coalition-Building Scheme

Between July 1970 and January 1973, the Alliance concluded coalition agreements with four former opposition parties: SUPP in Sarawak; Gerakan, the governing party in Penang; the PPP, which controlled the Ipoh Municipal Council in Perak; and PAS, which ruled the state of Kelantan. With the advent of these coalitions, only one major party in the peninsula remained in the opposition—the DAP. Although Tun Razak wanted a very broad coalition, UMNO elites could not abide the style and policies of the top DAP leaders and believed that there was no possibility they could work with them.

These coalitions had seemed inconceivable just a short time earlier, and many Malaysians were very surprised at the early coalition announcements. SUPP, a Chinese-dominated party, had opposed Malaysia, had joined Singapore's ill-fated united opposition movement, and was widely believed to have been deeply infiltrated by Communists. Gerakan, a multiethnic but primarily Chinese party, was led by Chief Minister Dr. Lim Chong Eu, the former president of the MCA who had been forced to resign in 1959 after antagonizing

UMNO during the "July crisis." The PPP, a non-Malay party
founded by two Sri Lankan brothers, had consistently and
loudly championed non-Malay language and education causes.
Finally, PAS, the Malay Islamic party, had long accused UMNO
of selling out the Malays by working and compromising with
non-Malay infidels, and by concentrating on material development at the expense of spiritual matters.

All of these party leaders were co-opted into coalitions
by a variety of incentives (and even veiled threats) such as
a chance to be in the government, thereby gaining respectability
and providing policy inputs; being named to government
bodies and for overseas posts; being put up for honors; and
being promised development funds for favorite projects. Furthermore, SUPP leaders obtained federal help in purging their
internal Communists, the shaky Gerakan government in Penang was propped up by Alliance support, the PPP was
assured that the Municipal Council would not be dissolved,
and the federal investigation into allegations of corruption
by PAS state leaders in Kelantan was dropped. Beyond this,
the opposition leaders were well aware of the new political
circumstances in the country and the fact that the issues upon
which they had most successfully campaigned were now
proscribed. Finally, Tun Razak was a superb coalition builder.
He was willing to let bygones be bygones and to sit down
with old and sometimes bitter foes—and he could deliver
what he promised.

The Formation of the Barisan Nasional

Starting in mid-1972, when a coalition with PAS seemed
likely, the speeches of Tun Razak made reference to the
concept, and at times even the existence, of a Barisan Nasional
(National Front). A period of confusion followed and questions
arose as to whether the Barisan was just a concept or whether
it was to have form and substance beyond the coalition
agreements. In September 1973, PAS President Datuk Asri
bin Haji Muda told newspaper reporters that "there is only
a coalition government, but it is moving towards a national
front. However, as there is no clear picture of a front yet, it
is premature to say" what the result will be.

In April 1974, in preparation for the general elections, Tun Razak announced that there would be a common symbol (the *dacing,* or scales of justice) for all Barisan Nasional parties in the elections. No individual party symbols would be allowed, and the Alliance sailing-boat symbol would be consigned to the museum.

In May, various Barisan rallies were held and the election slogan and Barisan manifesto were formulated. On June 1, 1974, the Barisan Nasional was officially registered with Tun Razak as the chairman. It originally consisted of nine parties: the UMNO, MCA, MIC, PAS, PPP, and Gerakan in Peninsular Malaysia; SUPP and the Malay/Melanau and Iban Parti Pesaka Bumiputera Bersatu (PBB) in Sarawak; and the Sabah Alliance (itself composed of the United Sabah National Organization [USNO], which was a Muslim party, and the Sabah Chinese Association). Tun Razak hailed the Barisan as "the climax of our political strategies in the 1970s."

The public response to the coalitions and the Barisan was widely favorable, but not all of the partners were happy about the developments. The MCA, especially, felt aggrieved that its historic role as sole representative of the Chinese was threatened (along with its seat allocations). The party had been undergoing a "revival," but disagreements over how to respond to the disliked coalitions had driven a sharp wedge between the "new bloods" and "old guards" and compounded the rivalry for internal power and position. By mid-1973 the "new bloods" had been defeated and most were expelled or had resigned from the party. In April 1974, long-time President Tun Tan Siew Sin, by now weary with the constant infighting, resigned and was succeeded by "old guard" stalwart, Datuk Lee San Choon. The MCA then tried to put forth a tough position, hinting that it might not stay with the government, but Tun Razak merely told the party that it must respond to "the winds of change." In the end, the MCA remained, although it was given fewer seats to contest and could no longer legitimately claim to be the sole representative of the Chinese. Since then, the MCA has been largely preoccupied with regaining its historic role, not only by defeating the DAP but also by undermining Gerakan and the PPP.

Another party unhappy with the Barisan was USNO (of the Sabah Alliance) under Chief Minister Tun Mustapha. He insisted on using his old party symbol instead of the *dacing*, and he declined to hold a state election in 1974. This was the beginning of a sharp deterioration of relations between Tun Razak and Tun Mustapha, which culminated in the ousting of the Sabah Alliance from the Barisan in 1975 (it was deemed to have withdrawn), federal backing for a rival multiethnic party, Berjaya, and Mustapha's fall from power in 1976.

The 1974 General Elections

The federal government held all the cards for the August 1974 general elections. The Malays were solidly united, Tun Razak's recent visit to China and meeting with Mao Zedong had greatly impressed the Malaysian Chinese, and the economy was bouncing back strongly after the inflationary effects of the Arab oil price increases. Moreover, these were the first general elections since the riots; campaign rallies had been banned, and it was expected that the voters would exercise caution. In the peninsula, the main opposition came from the DAP, which, within the limits allowed by the Sedition Act, tried to promote the Chinese language, education, and cultural causes and to air the grievances of the Chinese community in general. In Sarawak, the major challenge came from the Sarawak National party (SNAP), a multiethnic but basically Iban party that championed native interests and "Sarawak for the Sarawakians." In Sabah, the opposition was so repressed that only one opposition member managed to register his candidacy successfully.

As had been widely predicted, the results gave the Barisan Nasional a landslide parliamentary victory and clear control of all state assemblies. The Barisan won 104 of 114 parliamentary seats in Peninsular Malaysia and 31 of 40 seats from the Borneo states (in total, 135 of 154 parliamentary seats). The opposition consisted of the DAP (9 seats), SNAP (9 seats), and Pekemas, a peninsular multiethnic party (1 seat). No Malays sat in the opposition benches of Parliament.

SUCCESSION AND THE BREAKDOWN
OF MALAY UNITY

In the post-riot period, with Malay hegemony firmly established, the imperative for Malay ethnic solidarity began to lessen. There were no doubts that the Malays would govern; however, the "new realism" had the negative effect of facilitating the growth of factionalism, itself accompanied by a decline in Malay deference, which has characterized Malay politics since the mid-1970s.

Datuk Hussein Onn

In January 1976, Tun Razak died suddenly after a secret battle against leukemia. He was succeeded as prime minister by his deputy, Datuk (now Tun) Hussein Onn, the son of the first president of UMNO. Datuk Hussein, having already suffered a heart attack and in fragile health, found his administration embattled and plagued with party controversy, dissension, and challenges to his authority. An important coalition breakdown also occurred during his tenure in office.

One of Datuk Hussein's significant early actions was to name his deputy prime minister. He bypassed the senior UMNO vice-president to pick the man the Tunku had expelled from the party in 1969—namely, the controversial former "rebel," Dr. Mahathir Mohamad. This choice set in motion a major factional realignment of forces within UMNO. Because Datuk Hussein could not impose the same degree of political control as that wielded by the former prime minister, unprecedented political maneuvering and intrigue developed within the party.

A major blow to Datuk Hussein's authority resulted from his sponsorship of the expulsion from the party of Dato Harun bin Haji Idris, the powerful former *menteri besar* of Selangor and UMNO Youth president. Under indictment on corruption charges, Dato Harun was expelled from UMNO in March 1976 for ignoring advice to abstain from political activity. Although subsequently convicted, his expulsion was strongly opposed by the rank-and-file; under pressure, the

UMNO Supreme Council readmitted him to the party in October 1976 (apparently at the urging of Dr. Mahathir).

Coalition problems also surfaced between UMNO and PAS over what PAS believed were UMNO encroachments into its political territory in Kelantan. In 1977, the dispute between the two partners reached crisis proportions. When PAS voted in Parliament against the Emergency Powers (Kelantan) Bill in 1977 (an action deemed necessary because of public disturbances that had led to a PAS State Assembly no-confidence vote against the UMNO-backed Kelantan *menteri besar*), the Barisan Supreme Council ordered PAS to expel those who had defied the whip. PAS refused to comply and on December 16, 1977, all thirteen PAS MPs crossed the floor and PAS announced that it was now in opposition. As a result, UMNO once again faced the challenge of a party pushing Malay nationalist and Islamic demands unencumbered by the constraints of accommodation.

The 1978 General Elections

By the time of the July general elections, PAS, after nineteen years of rule, was still in shock over losing control of the state of Kelantan in the state election there of March 1978. The party responded by shifting its attention to Kedah and by trying to claim the leadership of the Islamic resurgence movement, then beginning to sweep the country. It promised to institute Islamic law in Kedah if it came to power.

The non-Malay opposition concentrated on the grievances of the non-Malays—specifically, those concerning employment, university admissions, and the restrictions imposed by the Industrial Coordination Act (ICA). The Barisan stuck to the middle ground, stressing development achievements and political stability. UMNO warned against incorrect interpretations of the Quran and criticized PAS for dividing the Malays. The non-Malay peninsular partners, while occasionally sabotaging each other's efforts, called for support so that they could defend non-Malay interests.

In Sarawak there was no major party in the opposition as SNAP had joined the Barisan in 1976, although some controversy did arise over the chief minister's management of the state. In Sabah, Barisan partners Berjaya and USNO (both having been admitted to the coalition in 1976 following Berjaya's state election victory over USNO in April) turned their wrath on one another through "friendly contests."

The 1978 election results gave the Barisan Nasional 131 of 154 parliamentary seats, with over 57 percent of the popular vote and control of all state assemblies. The opposition won 23 parliamentary seats, of which the DAP won 16 and PAS won 5 seats. PAS, despite the low number of seats it had won, still represented a formidable threat in the four northern states, winning about 40 percent of the total vote in seats contested. The DAP maintained its dominance of large urban constituencies, winning 12 of 13 contests in Peninsular Malaysia, whereas the non-Malay proportion of the electorate was higher than 70 percent. Overall, the general elections showed that the opposition was becoming increasingly concentrated in just two parties whose ethnic demands were completely incompatible.

A NEW LEADER: THE MAHATHIR ADMINISTRATION

In July 1981, Datuk Hussein resigned following a complicated triple bypass heart operation. His health was not sufficiently sound to meet the demands of the office or to bear the continuing stress resulting from various challenges to his authority by such UMNO stalwarts as Dato Harun (who was to be released from jail with a full pardon). Datuk Hussein's successor as prime minister was Datuk Seri Dr. Mahathir.

With UMNO party elections coming up, Dr. Mahathir prudently decided to await the results of the hotly contested UMNO deputy president race before naming his deputy prime minister (traditionally the UMNO deputy president is also the deputy prime minister). The contest was between Datuk Musa Hitam, a former "rebel" who had criticized Alliance policies after the 1969 riots and who was also viewed as Dr. Mahathir's choice, and the rich Kelantan prince, Tengku Razaleigh Hamzah, who was senior in the party hierarchy.

In a close finish, Datuk Musa won and was subsequently named deputy prime minister. Dr. Mahathir was unopposed as UMNO president. Normally this would have "settled" the issue of the top hierarchy, at least in terms of party challenges. But Tengku Razaleigh made it clear from the time of his defeat that he did not consider the mandate irrevocable.

The 1982 General Elections

As soon as the Mahathir administration had settled into office, outlined its programs and policies, and demonstrated its capabilities and enthusiasm for action, the government decided that it wanted a new electoral mandate. Early elections were called for April 1982.

The Barisan's election theme stressed its record of political stability, ethnic accord, and development, and it called for a strong government so that it could launch Malaysia's economic "take-off." The Malay campaign pitted UMNO against PAS, and the key issues concerned Islam and development. PAS called for a federal Islamic constitution and Islamic law, criticized UMNO's devotion to "secular" development, and warned of the danger of encroachments by the non-Malays. In some areas, PAS officials called UMNO members "infidels" and urged followers to pray at separate mosques. PAS, however, entered the campaign partially debilitated by a bitter internal power struggle between the "old guard" and the Islamic purist "young turks," who had recently been so eagerly recruited.

UMNO countered PAS attacks by emphasizing the numerous steps the government had taken, and planned to take, to promote Islam in the country. UMNO officials pointed out that economic development did not mean westernization, and that it needed to be matched by discipline, moral rectitude, and spiritual advancement. UMNO's biggest pre-election bonanza was its co-opting of former ABIM (Angkatan Belia Islam Malaysia, the Islamic Youth Movement) president, Encik Anwar Ibrahim, into the party. Prior to this, it had been feared in government circles that Anwar would either formally link ABIM with PAS or else would personally join PAS, possibly succeeding Datuk Asri as president. Anwar chose UMNO because of his close personal ties with Dr. Mahathir and also because he believed he could best accomplish his Islamic goals from within the government party.

Islam was not an issue in the non-Malay campaign. The issues there remained basically unchanged: unemployment, university admissions, economic and political discrimination. The difference this time was that some powerful and traditionally oppositional Chinese organizations, such as the United Chinese School Teachers Association, decided that their interests could be best defended from inside the government. The MCA, sensing that its appeal for Chinese unity was finding a better reception, decided to have some of the party elite contest in the urban DAP strongholds. MCA President Datuk Lee San Choon gave up his safe Johor seat to contest DAP-held Seremban (with a 78 percent non-Malay electorate), a move that won him much Chinese applause for his courage. By contrast, the DAP had been weakened by internal dissension and defections: Its leader, Lim Kit Siang, for a variety of reasons shied away from a direct contest with Datuk Lee in Seremban, and the DAP campaign seemed unusually disorganized and lethargic.

The election results gave the Barisan 132 of 154 parliamentary seats, with over 60 percent of the popular vote (the highest since independence), and control of all state assemblies. In Peninsular Malaysia, the Barisan won 103 of 114 parliamentary seats, losing only 5 seats to PAS and 6 to the DAP. To the surprise of many, the MCA and Gerakan were able to win over half of the 12 biggest urban seats (including Seremban). The voter swing in some constituencies was 30 percent or more. In Sabah, Berjaya won 10 of 11 contests (1 loss to the DAP), whereas 5 Berjaya-sponsored independents demolished the USNO candidates. In Sarawak, SNAP lost 3 seats to former disgruntled members running as independents, and SUPP lost 2 seats to the DAP (the Barisan won 29 of 40 parliamentary seats in Sabah and Sarawak).

The government viewed the election results as a strong endorsement of its policies, programs, and style. UMNO was succeeding in its efforts to "out-Islam" PAS. On the non-

The National Mosque in Kuala Lumpur. In the left corner is the railway station, and in the background, with the tower, are the Houses of Parliament. (Courtesy of the Ministry of Information, Malaysia.)

Malay side, the unanswered question concerned the motivation behind the sudden support for the old "Chinese unity" theme. Was it representative of genuine support, simple disillusionment with the efficacy of oppositional politics, or fear about the perceived trends of the new administration?

Islamization

In the 1970s, additional government measures to promote Islam came in response to the demands being made by the fundamentalist groups springing up in the country (see Chapter 4). The government sought to control and assume leadership of the Islamic resurgence so that UMNO would not become increasingly vulnerable to charges that it was promoting secularism. Government actions—such as sponsoring the annual Quran-reading competitions, building still more mosques, and instructing Malay ministers to wear their *songkoks* (Malay-Muslim hats) and attend mosque services—were largely symbolic (though still important). These measures were intended to raise the public profile of Islam and enhance its image without affecting the nation's basically secular political and economic systems.

A change has occurred in the time since Dr. Mahathir became the prime minister. Instead of just responding to Islamic pressures, the government has initiated a process of Islamization. The prime minister has stated on several occasions that he is not opposed to the establishment of an "Islamic state" (itself a vague concept), although he has always carefully added that Islam respects the rights of non-Muslims.[2] Among the government's major initiatives have been (1) the establishment of an Islamic bank and the International Islamic University, (2) a ban on the importation of non-*halal* beef (beef not slaughtered in accordance with Islamic rites), (3) greatly increased Islamic content on radio and television, (4) the reintroduction of *Jawi* (Arabic script) into the primary school curriculum, (5) the suspension of the government meal program in multiethnic national primary schools during the fasting month, (6) a ban on smoking in all government offices, and (7) amendments to the penal code and the criminal procedure code relating to religion, thereby giving the government rather Draconian powers to curb religious fanaticism.

By the latter part of 1982 and in early 1983 there were signs that the non-Malays, who had always treated Islam solely as a Malay concern, were becoming alarmed with the speed and extent of the Islamization process, especially as it threatened to touch them directly. Even some Malays were worried. At this point, however, the government retracted some contentious proposals. For example, a compulsory university Islamic civilization course was announced, and then, after concern was expressed, it was made optional for non-Muslims. Later, a federal minister announced that "morality laws" might be introduced to expose the public to aspects of Islamic law. The prime minister quickly reassured non-Muslims that such laws would not be implemented until extensive studies had been carried out, and in fact the proposal has been either shelved or dropped completely. By 1984, because UMNO was still responding to the basic concerns and fears of the non-Malays, the alarm over Islamization had been soothed.

UMNO has thus far managed to successfully "out-Islam" PAS without alienating the non-Muslims. But it could be boxing itself into the proverbial corner. PAS Islamic radicals have ousted the "old guard" and have upped their demands (they appear to admire Khomeini and the Iranian Islamic revolution). To keep the initiative from falling to PAS, UMNO may have to invoke measures that would directly impinge upon the fundamental freedoms and lifestyles of the non-Muslims. Consequently, there is a danger in the future that Islamization could negatively affect ethnic relations.

POLITICS, 1983–1985

Malaysia has one of the more open and competitive political systems in the region, and, despite a general preference by elites for reduced levels of "politicking," new or renewed crises and challenges regularly arise to stimulate political interest and, at times, to raise political temperatures. Recent years have been no exception; on the contrary, the numbing effects of the 1969 riots may be wearing off.

The Constitutional Crisis

A five-month constitutional crisis developed in 1983 following the July parliamentary passage of some constitutional amendments to which the *agung*, after consultation with the other rulers, refused to give his assent. He also refused to sign bills pertaining to government finances (supply) for 1984 and authorization for the new constituency boundaries. Ironically, the origin of the crisis was government concern over clarifying possible ambiguities with regard to the role of the constitutional monarch and the issue of "assent" by amending the constitution so that bills passed by Parliament could become law after a short delay even without the signature of the *agung*. The reasons behind the government's action were, first, that the likeliest candidates to become *agung* in 1984 were "independent-minded," and second, that in the

The *yang dipertuan agung*, Sultan Mahmood Iskandar Ibni Al-Marhum Sultan Ismail of Johor. He was elected by his fellow rulers to the five-year post in 1984. (Courtesy of the Ministry of Information, Malaysia.)

past some state rulers had refused to accept the advice of
menteris besar (or, in a few cases, even their appointment)
and had obstructed the enactment of Assembly bills.[3]

News of the impasse or "crisis" was not reported in the
Malaysian mass media for nearly four months—that is, until
former UMNO Minister Datuk Senu Abdul Rahman distributed copies of his "open letter" to the prime minister, and
the Tunku wrote about it in his column in *The Star.* At this
point, after failures at mediation, the government decided to
take its case directly to the people with a series of well-
publicized mass rallies. Even then, given Malay feelings of
loyalty and respect toward the rulers, the government was
careful to avoid impugning personalities (except for the occasional hint), and for the most part limited its case to
explaining the accepted concept of a *constitutional* monarchy
and the need for legal clarification of its position.

Although support for the government was probably not
so overwhelming as was reported in the mass media, it *was*
substantial—a fact that perhaps came as a surprise to the
rulers, who found they could not counter this campaign very
successfully. In mid-1984, unofficial estimates provided by
informed persons reckoned that the majority of Malays supported the government's position; however, it appeared that
many members of the Chinese business class supported the
rulers quite strongly, though silently. In December 1983, a
compromise was reached whereby the amendments and other
bills were signed into law on the understanding that a special
session of Parliament would be called to pass new amendments. Accordingly, the Constitution Amendment Act of 1984
voided two of the three 1983 amendments and changed the
other by lengthening the time the *agung* could legally delay
giving his assent before a bill became law.

At present, the crisis is officially concluded and the new
agung installed, but the issue is still "sensitive," ripples are
still being felt, and divisions are yet to be fully healed.

MCA Troubles

The MCA may have a subconscious "death wish." Yet
in the past it has survived reports that it was "more dead

than alive" and even some premature obituaries. In 1983–1984, a deep factional split left the MCA divided into two antagonistic camps. By mid-1985 the split had grown into a triangular contest.

The MCA's troubles started soon after President Datuk Lee San Choon's sudden and still unexplained resignation from his party post and the government in April 1983. Datuk Lee handpicked Datuk Dr. Neo Yee Pan as acting president rather than choosing to call a party election for the post. After several dismal MCA by-election losses, a faction led by business tycoon and MCA Vice-President Tan Koon Swan made clear its intention of challenging the acting leadership at the party elections scheduled originally for May 1984.

Each faction then maneuvered to get its own electoral delegates selected. When the Tan group accused the leadership of creating "phantom" members and obtained a court injunction to prevent divisional elections from proceeding, Tan and thirteen other high-ranking members were expelled from the MCA (two of them subsequently resigned their government positions as deputy ministers) in March 1984. Datuk Lee added to the intrigue by suddenly offering to mediate the dispute (some believe it was an attempt by him to regain power); but it became clear that he was backing the Tan group, and his efforts failed. The Tan group then organized an Extraordinary General Meeting, or EGM (held at the same time as the regular MCA anniversary assembly), which voted to reinstate the expelled members. The legality of the EGM was to be decided by the Malaysian High Court, and consequently party elections were postponed indefinitely.

On January 30, 1985, after a determined mediating effort by UMNO leaders, including the prime minister, the feuding factions of the MCA signed a "nobody loses" peace pact. Tan and his group were reinstated, but on the condition that they accept a predetermined list of office bearers for the next party elections. Moreover, all pending court cases were withdrawn, and a general meeting of the party was scheduled for May. However, in April a replay of the power struggle commenced, along with public accusations and the filing of a new series of lawsuits and injunctions. Another truce was arranged in May when both sides agreed to drop legal action and to establish a joint ad hoc committee, headed by UMNO stalwart Encik Ghafar Baba, to draw up accurate membership lists. In August 1985 the MCA acting president and labour minister, Datuk Mak Hon Kam, broke with Datuk Neo and set up his own splinter faction, thus dividing the MCA three ways. Also in August, Datuk Neo was dropped from the Cabinet—a clear indication of UMNO displeasure—and the Barisan Supreme Council issued an ultimatum, to which the MCA factions agreed, that the party would voluntarily exit from the Barisan if it had not resolved its problems in three months.

By the time of writing, in November 1985, the ad hoc committee had produced a "clean" membership list (although the Mak and Neo groups had accused the Tan group, which gained access to the master list, of tampering with the disk), and MCA branch and divisional elections were taking place. An MCA general assembly was scheduled for November 24, 1985, at which time elections could finally decide the leadership struggle.

However, the factional struggle, widely and cynically viewed as a battle for personal gain, has disenchanted and embarrassed many in the Chinese community. Even if the leadership issue is resolved, the struggle has generated so much rancor and ill will that it will be very difficult to reunite the party short of having the losers withdraw or be expelled from the party. Just after the MCA's outstanding performance in the 1982 general elections, some party insiders conceded that it was a feat that might prove impossible to duplicate. Now the party must worry that it may fare significantly worse at the next general elections.

The 1984 UMNO General Assembly

As has been widely remarked, there are good reasons for considering the triennial UMNO General Assembly elections as Malaysia's "real elections." First, they are important inasmuch as the party's leaders assume the top government positions. Second, the UMNO party elections are in many ways more open and "democratic" than the general elections, partly because anyone nominated by even one of the 114 divisions for a position can contest, but more generally because it is an intraethnic affair conducted by the dominant group, and the government has not been as tough about "do's and don'ts" as it is during a general election when ethnic violence must be considered. Of late, especially, these elections have started to take on the style of U.S. party conventions; huge sums of money are spent on lengthy and well-organized campaigns (including posters, buttons, glossy color résumés, promises of all kinds, perquisites, and outright vote buying). Malaysians nowadays talk about "how much" it is worth to become an UMNO divisional chairperson (presumably because of his or her influence over the votes of the other delegates from the division). The reason for all this is that the stakes are high. There tends to be a direct correlation between high party position and a high government post. An exception would be an efficient minister with political ambitions but without grassroots strength—for example, Tan Sri Ghazali Shafie, who left the cabinet in 1984. Another possible exception is Encik Daim Zainuddin, a business tycoon who became a member of Parliament in 1982 and minister of finance in 1984. It is conceivable that Daim may try to cultivate a political base, in which case he will need to perform well at the next party elections. But it seems more likely that, as a close confidant of the prime minister, he will be content to operate as a technocrat, wielding influence through advice rather than seeking power via the grass roots.

With the possible exception of the very top leader, there has been a steady erosion of deference toward incumbents. In May 1984, this meant that the deputy president was challenged, nine contested for the three regular vice-president posts, and forty-eight vied for the twenty elected Supreme Council seats.

Quite naturally, the most prominent contest was between Deputy President Datuk Musa Hitam and his challenger, Tengku Razaleigh, the minister of finance. Musa had defeated Razaleigh in 1981, and shortly thereafter both began quietly campaigning for the expected rematch. There were some differences in 1984. The prime minister had stated directly this time that he wanted Musa as number two (so directly, in fact, that at the 1983 UMNO General Assembly he was booed by some delegates and generally criticized).[4] Another difference was that Musa was the incumbent with all of the resources of incumbency. Third, the election followed on the heels of the constitutional crisis, and Musa and Razaleigh were sometimes perceived as representing opposing loyalist-royalist positions. Finally, the occupational background composition of the delegates was different: There was a sharp decline in the percentage of teachers and a corresponding increase in the number of businessmen. In 1981, this composition would have been viewed as helpful to Razaleigh, but by 1984 Musa's support from the teachers had supposedly declined while his influence within the business sector had risen.

The election results gave Musa 744 and Razaleigh 501 votes (despite the different circumstances, these results were very close to the 1981 figures of 722 to 517, respectively). The third (last-minute) candidate, the once powerful Dato Harun, received only 34 votes. The results showed that Razaleigh had a solid and substantial block of votes. He has had to pay a price for challenging and losing, but he remains too powerful to be politically "finished off." In July 1984, he was shifted to the less prestigious but still politically powerful portfolio of minister of trade and industry, was dropped as party treasurer and chairman of Kelantan state UMNO, and, surprisingly, was not one of the six appointed by the president to the Supreme Council.

The contests for the vice-president and Supreme Council positions were remarkable for the number of new members elected: 2 out of 3 for vice-president and 11 out of 20 for the Supreme Council. The most significant victory was that of Datuk Abdullah Badawi for vice-president and his subsequent appointment as minister of education (a portfolio that is popularly viewed as leading eventually to the prime ministership). He is now a strong contender for the number-three spot in the succession line-up, his chief rival being fellow Penangite Encik Anwar Ibrahim, president of UMNO Youth and minister of agriculture.

It is clear from the 1984 UMNO elections that the influence of the educated Malay business class is on the rise, patronage and big money politics are growing, and deference, along with any sense of complacency an incumbent may once have felt, is declining. UMNO is successfully overcoming one of the traditional problems that plague dominant parties, that of leadership renewal. Many new people are finding a place in the hierarchy; indeed, the speed with which the younger generation is replacing the old guard is considered alarming by some, not all of whom constitute the old guard. The average age of the UMNO hierarchy (Supreme Council or higher) is just over forty years. If the present trend continues and is not checked by effective curbs on party election excesses, UMNO elections in the future can be expected to be more costly and intense; their outcomes may be less predictable, and the turnover might adversely affect UMNO's traditional stability.

The 1985 Sabah State Election

One of Malaysia's biggest political surprises in the past several years occurred in April 1985 when a seven-week-old party, Parti Bersatu Sabah (PBS), won a majority of seats in the Sabah state election over the ruling Berjaya party and the latter's arch-rival, USNO. The PBS, under founder-president Datuk Joseph Pairin Kitingan, won 25 seats (and almost immediately added an additional seat when the only winner of the United Pasok Nunukragang National Organization defected to the PBS). Berjaya, which had held 44 of the 48 elected seats, won only 6 seats, and its president, Chief Minister Datuk Harris Salleh, lost his contest to a political unknown. Equally surprising in the election was the revival of Tun Mustapha's USNO party, which captured 16 seats. USNO came into the election holding only 3 seats, and it had been expelled from the Barisan in April 1984 for its breach of discipline concerning the constitutional crisis. Many forecasters had already prepared its obituary.

Berjaya's sharp decline can most likely be traced to the public perception that the party had become arrogant and that it was making inefficient use of public funds.[5] Furthermore Berjaya could not escape being associated with the much-resented intrusion of over 300,000 Filipino, Indonesian, and Pakistani immigrants. Of course, the election had a significant ethnic dimension as well. The PBS appealed to Kadazans and Catholics and won most of the pivotal Chinese vote, whereas USNO captured most of the Muslim vote. Purportedly, multiethnic Berjaya (which has in fact been pro-Muslim under Datuk Harris) was left with the residual votes.

The surprise elicited by the election results (mainly because the PBS was less than two months old) was accompanied by a sense of déja vu: From almost one-party rule, USNO had fallen from power in 1976 under similar circumstances—dethroned by the new Berjaya party.

Malaysians were still reacting to the election results when even more startling news was broadcast: A USNO-Berjaya coalition had been formed and Tun Mustapha had been sworn in as chief minister. Apparently Tun Mustapha and Datuk Harris had convinced the governor that their combined 22 seats, plus the 6 nonelected seats that a chief minister is entitled to appoint after he is sworn in, would give then a majority of 28 out of a total of 54 seats. However, Datuk Musa Hitam, the acting prime minister, reacted swiftly by denouncing the power grab and calling for Sabahans to remain calm. When Datuk Harris telephoned to inform him about the idea, he said that he had rejected the plot because it thwarted the will of the people.[6] Several hours later, the governor terminated Tun Mustapha's tenure as chief minister and swore in the leader of the PBS, Datuk Pairin.

Throughout 1985 the PBS expanded its assembly seat holdings through defections to it. Also, in October the party won a parliamentary by-election contest against Berjaya, thus raising its total in Parliament to three (the previous two having come to the PBS as the result of crossovers). Nevertheless, the political situation in Sabah remains fluid and tense. In mid-1985 bombings rocked the capital of Kota Kinabalu and raised suspicions that the perpetrators might be trying to create a climate conducive to having the federal government impose emergency rule over the state in the name of national security. Also in mid-year, Tun Mustapha filed a civil suit challenging the governor's discretionary powers to invalidate his tenure as chief minister (scheduled to be heard in court in December 1985). This suit was followed by a spate of other lawsuits and injunctions intended to disrupt and destabilize the PBS government. In November, Berjaya and USNO decided to apply further pressure on the PBS by acting on the undated resignations of four assemblymen, three of whom had defected to the PBS. (It has been a standard if questionable practice in Sabah to have elected assemblymen sign undated letters of resignation which can be invoked by the party leader at any time.) The four by-elections, in opposition strongholds, scheduled for January 1986, could cut into the majority of the PBS.

Further complicating the scene is the fact that a number of UMNO elites are uncomfortable with the PBS. Some consider Datuk Pairin a "Catholic chauvinist," and some have accused Datuk Pairin of an anti-Muslim bias in his reshuffling of the civil service.[7] With general elections on the horizon, UMNO does not want to provide ammunition to PAS by being seen as defending and/or accepting a Christian party while pro-Muslim parties sit in the opposition. Consequently, PBS overtures to join the Barisan have been rejected to date; instead the federal government is believed to be pressuring for a state coalition government comprised of the three contending parties.

SUMMARY

In this chapter we have seen that since the time of independence, and especially since the May 1969 riots, the Malays gradually but increasingly asserted their political dominance. To a large extent they can, as Dr. Mahathir has suggested, control their own destinies. But as the Malay elite well understands, they cannot hope to be completely successful in any of their endeavors if in the process they seriously alienate large sections of the non-Malay minority. Accordingly, the UMNO Malays have continued the practice of ethnic accommodation and power sharing, albeit within limits set by them, to ensure Malay dominance.

4

The Society: Ethnicity, Class, and Culture

A description of Malaysia's social structure and social life must include certain obvious features: basic data on population; ethnicity, including language and religion; social class; life in the countryside and the problem of rural poverty; urbanization; and changes in the towns. Beyond these, the most important are education, the mass media, interest groups, and the role of women. The last sections of this chapter are devoted to these themes.

POPULATION

The size of a country's population places constraints on its policy options. Its ability to defend territory, the size of its labor force, the extent of its internal market, and the like all depend on population size. Malaysia's 1984 population was roughly 15 million. In Peninsular Malaysia, during the period 1957–1976, fertility dropped by more than 40 percent, whereas life expectancy at birth rose by 16 percent for males and 25 percent for females. As in many other developing countries, until very recently the emphasis has been on reducing fertility, mainly through the activities of the National Family Planning Board, although the current population growth rate is still higher than the Board's target of 2 percent for the mid-1980s. The Sabah rate has been much higher because of substantial immigration from the Philippines and Indonesia.

However, the direction of population policy was called into question, and then reversed, by the prime minister's announcement that the expansion of the manufacturing sector required a large internal market, possibly 70 million by the year 2100. As an initial step, he announced in 1984 that maternity leave and benefits for mothers working in government service would be available for the first five children, not, as previously, for the first three, and tax benefits for up to five children were announced in the 1985 budget. In response to the criticism that such a large population would require an expanded social infrastructure, especially for education and health services, he emphasized that hard work would be necessary in order to achieve the new goal. Another criticism is that this population target will be reached before 2100 without a rise in the economic growth rate.

ETHNICITY

Given the central role of ethnicity, there is this additional question about Malaysia's population: not just "how many?" but "how many of each ethnic group?" If, for instance, population projections indicated that the Malays were likely to become a minority in Peninsular Malaysia in the near future, these projections would have important political repercussions because of the consequent Malay feelings of insecurity.

In fact, the figures and trends for Peninsular Malaysia show that early substantial changes in ethnic proportions are unlikely. The present (approximate) percentages are these: Malays, 55 percent; Chinese, 34 percent; and Indians, 10 percent. There is a tiny percentage of "others," including the Eurasians, who seemed so prominent and so glamorous in the pages of such writers as Joseph Conrad and Somerset Maugham. The picture in the Borneo states is more complex, however. In Sarawak the Chinese constitute 29 percent of the population; the Ibans, as the largest indigenous group, constitute 30 percent; and the rest are nearly all indigenous. According to the 1980 census, Sabah's population is 16 percent Chinese and 83 percent *pribumi* (indigenous). In fact, about

Dressed in native attire, a couple from Sabah are about to begin a traditional dance (Tarian Sumazau). (Courtesy of Datuk Rais Yatim and the Malaysian Ministry of Information.)

a fifth of the latter are recent Filipino and Indonesian immigrants. Projections for Peninsular Malaysia indicate that the proportion of Malays is slightly increasing. They now have a higher fertility rate than that of the Chinese or Indians, whereas before 1957 their rate was lower; during the same period their mortality rate has also dropped more sharply. Population trends therefore do not constitute a threat to the politically dominant Malays.

Given the close correlation between being Malay and being Muslim in Peninsular Malaysia, Malay percentages are not very different from Muslim percentages. Muslims constitute just over 53 percent of the Malaysian population and consist of Malays and a few others, mostly Indians and Pakistanis, in Peninsular Malaysia; just over half the Sabah population; and a little over a quarter of the Sarawak population. Most Chinese practice a religion that contains elements of Confucianism and Buddhism, while the majority of Indians are Hindus. Some members of both groups are Christians. Those indigenous people in Sarawak and Sabah who are not Muslims are predominantly Christian, although some have no, or only a primitive form of, religion.

Ethnicity: Modernization

The figures for the aforementioned ethnic groups do not tell the whole story. Ethnicity is not an easily definable term— or, rather, it is *too* easily defined in too many different ways. At one time, for example, the aborigines in Peninsular Malaysia, numbering almost 100,000, were counted separately in the census; now they are included among "Malays." Under British rule, some of the censuses in Sabah showed huge changes over ten years in the numbers of various groups, the explanation being that the census-takers were given different instructions in different years about how to ask questions on, and classify, ethnicity. Beyond that, however, the main groups listed are by no means uniform. Even today, various versions of Malay are spoken in different states. There are several major Chinese dialect groups in Malaysia (Hokkien, Cantonese, Hakka, Teochew, Hainanese, and, in Sarawak, Foochow) as well as a few Indian ones (the main one being Tamil). The categories used for Sarawak and Sabah in the summary just given conceal a wealth of differences. The Ibans in Sarawak, for example, are martial and aggressive, quite unlike the Punans of the deep interior, who until recently lived very simply, almost totally unaffected by outside influences. In Sabah the Kadazans, numbering only about 200,000, were grouped a few years ago by an anthropologist into as many as fifteen separate varieties. An established category in Sarawak, the "Malays," refers to people who are from the same stock as some of their neighbors, but who, although not immediately related to the Malays in the peninsula, called themselves by that name when they were converted to Islam during the last few centuries.

Broad stereotypes regarding ethnic occupations are misleading. An image of the Chinese as traders and hawkers has to be accompanied by the supplementary knowledge that many of them are farmers. There may be great variations in customs and ways of life. Article 160 of the constitution uses conformity to "Malay custom" as part of the definition of a Malay. But Husin Ali pertinently asks whether a Malay officer who has an English wife, speaks English at home, eats at a table using fork and spoon, drinks beer, wears pajamas in bed, and has his daughter married at the Hilton hotel can properly, by this criterion, be called a Malay.[8] Conversely, he mentions the *Baba* (the Chinese in the Straits Settlements), who adopted Malay ways to the extent of speaking the language, singing Malay songs, eating cross-legged on the floor using their fingers, and marrying their children according to Malay ceremonies.

Nevertheless, although the finer points of ethnicity defy any simple summary, in a direct and crude form the ethnic divisions in the society closely affect people's lives. They can even put an end to their lives, as shown by the ethnic riots in Kuala Lumpur in May 1969 and a few other minor ethnic incidents. Exactly why does ethnicity assume such importance in a country like Malaysia? First, the cleavages—racial appearance, language, religion, and so on—are either readily apparent or have to do with issues or practices that people care about deeply. Second, the importance of these issues is illustrated by the fact that politicians find that people respond to them; if there were no political "market" for them, political leaders would not continue to use them. Dato Onn found this to be the case when he tried to attract support away

from UMNO and other ethnic parties by founding the Independence of Malaya party. Even today the most successful
parties, although they are components of the multiethnic
Barisan, have an ethnic base. It would be wrong to think
that modernization (which includes such processes as urbanization, industrialization, mass education, rising expectations,
and so forth) will necessarily make these divisions, and popular
reaction to them, out of date. Indeed, modernization—by
bringing into close proximity groups that previously had little
to do with each other, in the context of more competition
for jobs, scholarships, and so on—actually tends to exacerbate
ethnicity. The groups now have *economic* interests to fight
for, as well as religious and cultural ones. Competition is
modified to some extent by the guidelines set in the New
Economic Policy (discussed in Chapter 6). But the very fact
that the policy has been conceived in terms of ethnicity,
dividing the whole population into either Malays and other
indigenous people or non-Malays, greatly intensifies ethnic
perceptions.

In Malaysia and a few other countries, ethnicity also
has special political implications. The numbers of Malays and
non-Malays are approximately equal, so in the early days of
independence non-Malays in Malaya plausibly could have
speculated on the possibility of gaining power through the
ballot box, if their numbers had increased faster than the
Malay numbers. In fact these expectations were unrealistic.
But the possibility was enough to arouse fear among the
Malays and to encourage ethnic tensions.

What is happening now to the divisions and cleavages
that separate ethnic groups? Until recently, the different
communities did not come into contact very much but, instead,
were residentially segregated; in the rural areas they lived,
for the most part, in separate villages, and there were few
Malays in the towns. It was alleged that the British pursued
a policy of "divide and rule," but it is doubtful that the
various ethnic groups really wanted to see much more of
each other. In fact, the weakness in British arithmetic lay in
addition rather than in division, in the sense that the British
allowed large-scale immigration without figuring out what

the effects would be, especially after independence. Given the current tendency of people, especially Malays, to move to the towns, there is now probably less ethnic segregation there than before. But even when Malays relocate to a town, they are usually still segregated, inasmuch as they tend to group together in what significantly are called *kampungs* (villages), such as *Kampung Melayu* and *Kampung Java* in Kuala Lumpur. The observation has also been made that in the towns more Malays than Chinese are to be found in Malay-operated coffee shops, whereas the reverse is true of Chinese-operated coffee shops. Furthermore, there tend to be ethnic clusters at particular tables.

Apart from its economic implications, the importance of ethnicity in Malaysia is best appreciated by considering how the Malays' concern about their identity has been expressed in their attitudes and policies on language and religion.

Language

The Malays' fears for, and sense of insecurity about, the survival of their culture have led to a siege mentality in the face of perceived threats; they have also been the prime factor motivating Malay political goals and actions. Constitutional protection and political dominance, especially since the riots of May 13, 1969, have partly assuaged these fears, as has progress toward adopting significant segments of the Malay tradition into the culture defining the nation. Before this, in the 1950s and 1960s, one of the major preoccupying struggles concerned language. In 1957, as part of the Bargain, Malay became the official language (except that for ten years English retained equal status). After the 1969 riots, the pace of implementation was stepped up, and by stages Malay became the sole language of instruction in secondary and tertiary education. By the early 1970s, Malay was quite widely spoken by the non-Malays and this trend has continued, especially among younger people. The Chinese fought a successful rear-guard action when they managed to preserve free primary schooling in Chinese, but they lost the battle to set up a Chinese university. It took longer for Malay to become established in the Borneo territories, especially Sarawak. Even by 1984 it was said that only 10 percent of the civil servants there were using the language properly in their daily duties. In Peninsular Malaysia, however, the focus of attention has turned away from the question of how many people use it to differences of opinion about which usages are correct. Renamed *Bahasa Malaysia*, it rapidly became more complex through the coining of new terms and changes resulting from standardization with the closely related *Bahasa Indonesia*. It is estimated that the language agency in Malaysia coined as many as 175,000 new terms between 1957 and 1982! Concurrently, however, variations in spelling and usage continued to multiply.

Ironically, the language issue has had an unanticipated side effect. Although widespread usage ensured the perpetuation of the Malay language, it lost its "Malayness" in the process; as a result, a significant ethnic barrier, important to the preservation of Malay identity, was eroded. At the same time, other political initiatives, intended to help the Malays economically, have contributed to a new sense of Malay insecurity. As part of the New Economic Policy, Malay urbanization, business participation, and expanded university enrollments were encouraged. Malays new to the city, new Malay entrepreneurs, and large numbers of village Malays enrolled in domestic and overseas universities all found themselves exposed to life in busy, Western-oriented, competitive, and aggressive urban environments, where Malays, culturally and numerically, were distinctly in the minority. The resultant "culture shock" and renewed perceptions of the erosion of ethnic boundaries prompted a strong desire to enhance and protect Malay distinctiveness.

Religion

Islam, always a key ingredient of Malay cultural identity, has created the last and most impenetrable ethnic barrier; moreover, because it was perceived in ethnic rather than universal terms, it accentuated divisions between the Muslim portion of Malaysia's population (53 percent in 1980) and the rest. Historically and at present, Islam, more than any other cultural component, has impeded the integration of the non-Malays into Malay society, although in Sarawak and Sabah the situation is more fluid. This impediment arises not just because non-Malays are reluctant to convert. In recent decades, and as a by-product of Malay nationalism, not even conversion to Islam, by the Chinese especially, has served to bridge the cultural gulf to any great extent. Rather, it has led to the unofficial creation of a special class of Muslims who are sometimes encouraged to pray at separate mosques. The Malays still feel more kinship with their Arab brothers than with Malaysian converts.

Islam has been an integral part of Malay culture for five hundred years. However, it has mixed with, rather than displaced, important pre-Islamic traditions and beliefs, including Hindu political notions of feudal society rigidly demarcated between ruler and subject and governed by strict deference to rank. At the lowest level there was the village religious teacher running the Islamic school (such as the rural *pondok* schools, a particular type of religious school set up independently as a result of new land settlement by a migrant group that had attached itself to a religious teacher). There was also the local *imam* (religious functionary), who oversaw religious observances. These were linked through rules, rituals, and obligations—such as *fatwa* (Islamic legal rulings) and the collection of tithes—to the Islamic judges (*kadis*) and courts, who worked closely with the influential *ulamak* (religious scholars), who, in turn, formed councils to advise the rulers on religious matters. The result was a hierarchical network of religious functionaries (i.e., an informal "clergy"), operating to protect Islam and *adat* (customary law) and committed to the preservation of the feudal-like institutions of governance. This system was continued, and even strengthened, under the British.

The renewed interest, beginning in the early 1970s, in promoting Islam has led to some clashes between adherents of traditional Islamic practices and proponents of a purist and more fundamentalist interpretation of Islamic teachings. The Malaysian Islamic revival has been greatly influenced by the Islamic resurgence sweeping the Muslim world, itself fired by Arab oil money, by the Iranian Islamic revolution, and by a prophecy that foretold a glorious new Islamic era beginning in the Muslim year of 1400 (November 1979). Islam is a complete way of life, recognizing no legitimately distinct secular sphere of activity, and is governed by a complex set of rules and obligations. Generally, fundamentalists believe that no Muslim can be completely true to Islam unless he or she goes beyond ritual observances and lives in an Islamic polity complete with Islamic legal and economic systems. Consequently, the usual goal of fundamentalists is the establishment of an "Islamic state," the procedural content of which remains vague and undefined; the basic problem is to rationalize the sixth-century Arabian ideal to conform to the requirements of a modern state.

In Malaysia, fundamentalism has taken the form of the spread of a *dakwah* (meaning "to call") movement. It is not directed toward converting nonbelievers but, rather, is aimed toward making born Muslims better Muslims by stressing ritual and by trying to eliminate the accretions that have crept into Islamic practices. *Dakwah* is not one movement but many, ranging from small communal cults to large politically motivated groups, from extremists to moderate militants. Within *dakwah*, there are many variations in practices and in interpretations of the Quran. For example, the members of one small group, *Darul Arqam*, founded in 1969, live in a commune near Kuala Lumpur, wear Arab robes and veils, are absorbed with ritual, and try to follow exactly the ways of the Prophet. Another group, ABIM (the Islamic Youth Movement of Malaysia), which was formed in August 1971 and has about 35,000 members, is less concerned with ritual observance. ABIM seeks changes in government policy to allow for a complete Islamic way of life (*al-din*), or an "Islamic state," in Malaysia. Its leaders have not publicly proclaimed the structure or form of this Islamic society, but they have stated that its creation should be evolutionary and with due (unspecified) respect for the rights of the non-Muslims. Some of the economic grievances of the Malays, and even the non-Malays, find expression in ABIM pronouncements, which champion the poor and advocate mildly socialist solutions. ABIM has branches in every state, runs schools and cooperatives, publishes a magazine, and maintains links with several Arab nations. Originally its main following consisted of Western-educated middle-class urban Malay youth. It was led until late March 1982 by a charismatic former student "radical" concerned with social justice, Encik Anwar Ibrahim, who was then co-opted into the government. Since then, ABIM has toned down its demands and has adopted a "wait and see" policy concerning government Islamization initiatives. However, some of ABIM's top leaders are apparently working closely with PAS, and it appears that ABIM has been attracting increasing numbers of more militant Arabic-educated Malay youth.

Some small extremist groups have appeared as well. One such group desecrated a few Hindu temples in August 1978, while another raided a police station in October 1980 (both causing deaths); yet another organization, called "Crypto," even had its own flag and printed its own banknotes before it was broken up by the police in 1982. Still another extremist group that has operated in Kedah and Perlis is P.A.S. (Pertubuhan Angkatan Sabilullah, the Organization of the Forces of the Righteous Path), not to be confused with the Islamic party, PAS, although the government has claimed that some members of the latter belong to the former. Its goal is the creation of an "Islamic state," and it condones violence as a means. Formed in October 1978, it was apparently involved with the farmers' demonstration in Kedah in January 1980, at which time a number of its members were arrested. Violence involving an Islamic extremist group seeking to set up an Islamic state by force occurred in November 1985 near the Thai border. Police seeking to arrest the leader met with armed resistance. Eighteen were killed, including four policemen and the fundamentalist leader.

Although the extremists are an embarrassment to the government, they are not a threat. ABIM has prodded the Malay-led government to respond to Islamic demands. The government has feared a linkup between primarily urban ABIM and the rural and increasingly religiously militant Islamic party, PAS, and subsequently a wooing of the traditional and conservative Malay peasantry to the fundamentalist cause. To date, the linkup has been sporadic and the wooing only mildly successful.

Despite the resistance by rural Malays to demands to purify their Islamic practices, there is nonetheless a strong attraction to the power and pride of the Islamic resurgence, which the government decided could not be left to the manipulation or exploitation of the opposition Islamic parties or to unregulated *dakwah* activities, or even entirely to the control of individual state rulers. The government has been compelled to respond to Islamic demands; the result has been a process of Islamization (described in Chapter 3), which not only has made the country much more Islamic in character but has also acted vigorously to maintain ethnic boundaries.

SOCIAL CLASS

The importance of ethnicity in Malaysia largely accounts for the absence of any class divisions strong enough to produce substantial social or political effects. In a sense, class divisions have been preempted by ethnic divisions. Some exponents of class interpretations go further, saying that the "ruling classes" have conspired to encourage ethnic divisions in order to postpone the day when class divisions will unfold as they should. This assumption seems to be somewhat farfetched, however, if only because the ethnic divisions are so powerful that they hardly need any encouragement.

There are also historical reasons, as far as the Malays are concerned, for the very few visible divisions in the past between those who ruled and those who were ruled, and the complete absence of mass revolts. Rulers and chiefs were accorded respect and loyalty in a feudal kind of way, just as there was widespread respect for age, certain personal qualities, education, prestigious occupations, and wealth—a respect that formed an integral part of the all-pervading influence of *adat*. To some extent these attitudes are still influential. They are evident in the deference accorded to the rulers, in the fact that the first four leaders of UMNO were of high birth, and (until very recently) in the respectful behavior of delegates at UMNO general assemblies. They are also perpetuated, in a lower key, by the annual honors lists of awards (usually more than 2,000 a year), conferred with great ceremony by the *agung* and by each of the individual rulers.

However, contemporary "class" theories of politics are based on the primacy of economic relations, particularly the way in which certain groups are related to the mode of production. Apart from the persistence of respect, according to class theorists, differences between groups will inevitably assume forms that are primarily economically based.

It is quite easy to construct schemes along these lines that postulate the existence of classes among the Malays. The New Economic Policy has created a number of rich Malay business people, many of aristocratic descent; a Malay middle class consisting of civil servants and professional people; and a lower class made up of peasants and, increasingly, of Malay workers. In addition, as discussed later in this chapter, there is widespread poverty among the peasants. Such categories are plausible because they are paralleled by large differences in income. But the vital question is this: Are these differences accompanied by divisions that cause certain groups to resent other groups and to blame them for their own poverty and lack of opportunity? This question cannot properly be brushed aside by the class theorists' claim that ethnic tensions constitute an example of "false consciousness," or rather a lack of class consciousness, that, according to their assumptions, "ought" to exist. In fact, research indicates that, although poorer Malays do perceive that some Malay groups rank higher than others in wealth and status, few take the further step of resenting the existence of basic social inequalities. Conflicts between Malay individuals are not explicitly seen in class terms. Where economic injustice is perceived, the impulse is to look for an ethnic reason. In one instance, Malay consumers felt that a gas station was exploiting them by overcharging on gas prices, but they refused to believe that it was owned by Malays, as was the case, and not by Chinese.[9]

Lack of class consciousness among Malay peasants is partly attributable to other factors. Linked to the traditional influence of respect is the "patron-client" relationship between two persons. The patron supplies help, financially or by intervening to protect clients from the rigidity of bureaucratic rules. The client provides respect, services at feasts, and possibly electoral support. Since independence, the patron may in effect often perform the role of broker, allocating resources that are not his own but that he distributes on behalf of the government. Ties of kinship may also serve to moderate conflict, notably between landlords and tenants.

In spite of these considerations, two well-publicized expressions of peasant dissatisfaction have occurred in Kedah within the last few years: one in Baling in 1974 and the other in Alor Setar in 1980. In the first instance, prices for the principal crop, rubber, had dropped sharply, and there was considerable hunger, although claims of death from starvation were unsubstantiated. Farmers demonstrated and were joined by students, many of whom were ideologically motivated. As far as the farmers were concerned, hunger was the spur, not ideology, although if government help had not been forthcoming, ideological explanations might have come to appeal to them. More mysterious, however, was the Alor Setar affair, in which 15,000 people, mostly rice farmers, demonstrated and made attacks on state buildings. The harvest had been good and the government subsidy had been raised. The occasion for the demonstration was the introduction of a "coupon subsidy" scheme, designed to compel farmers to make forced savings, thereby helping them accumulate capital. The government was greatly surprised by the farmers' hostile reaction, which it alleged had been prompted by subversive organizations. To be sure, such organizations may have taken advantage of the situation, but the principal cause seems rather to have been the failure of certain government organizations to explain what the scheme was about. Although the government saw the scheme as benefiting the farmers, to them it looked like a deprivation.

Hence, neither of these indications of dissatisfaction, although each had a great impact at the time, upsets the generalization that class consciousness and organizations based on class have been relatively weak in Malaysia. But apart from these instances, given the relative quiescence of the peasantry, the most aggressive manifestations of discontent appear to come from the middle class, primarily as a result of the dissatisfaction of young people unable to find jobs commensurate with their educational qualifications. After independence the civil service provided good opportunities for upwardly mobile Malays, as, later, did government organizations such as PERNAS (Perbadanan Nasional, or State Trading Corporation) and private business under the stimulus of the New Economic Policy. There is still a demand for qualified Malay managers and entrepreneurs. But during the depression of the early 1980s, the positions available in both the public and private sectors were reduced. Apparently, at least 10 percent of new graduates may be spending up to a year or more looking for a job.

Less research has been done on class consciousness among the Chinese. A few, those who form the core of the small number of Marxist insurgents (see Chapter 7), are indeed extreme examples of the operation of class consciousness. But in the Malaysian context, the majority of the urban Chinese are either owners of small businesses or the people who work for small businesses, to whom they are linked by family ties or membership in the same dialect group. Some, employed by larger organizations, may be shy about joining trade unions because of the ill-fated backing some unions gave to the rebels during the "Emergency" and the current government restrictions on unions. Indians, on the other hand, are active in trade unions and provide a high proportion of the leaders. One study of Chinese and Indian perceptions found that both groups generally accorded wealth and business a higher status than did the Malays. But the concept of class was poorly understood, except by some of the more highly educated people.

Organizations that seek to bridge ethnic barriers on the basis of appeals to class have not made much headway. This has been true of the trade unions thus far, although the situation may change as the number of urban Malays increases. The only political party (apart from the early Independence

Mechanical harvesting of rice (*padi*) in Kuala Muda, Kedah. It is still not unusual, however, to see water buffalo in the fields doing the work of machines. (Courtesy of the Ministry of Information, Malaysia.)

of Malaya Party) that has attempted to act as a "bridge," the Socialist Front, foundered on an ethnic issue.

VILLAGE LIFE: PEASANTS AND POVERTY

As in most developing countries, the peasantry remains large as well as basically traditional and conservative despite the effects of modernization. In Peninsular Malaysia approximately 65 percent of the population is defined as rural, with a slightly higher percentage in Sabah and Sarawak. Rural dwellers (broadly speaking, the peasantry) include farmers, especially *padi* (rice) cultivators, rubber smallholders, and other agriculturalists, fishermen, cattle raisers, and handicraft producers. There is, of course, no such thing as a "typical" Malaysian village. Much depends on location—for example, on whether the village is situated on the west coast of Peninsular Malaysia or on the less developed east coast. In Sarawak and Sabah, the whole pattern of settlement is different, being more dispersed with very limited road networks. In Sarawak, some indigenous people still live in longhouses, which, originally built for defense, contain shared accommodations as well as separate family living quarters. Throughout Malaysia, moreover, are villages inhabited chiefly by nonindigenous people, including the "New Villages" for Chinese set up during the Emergency. But the Chinese, especially, find it hard to satisfy their need for land, because Malay attachment to the land is expressed in the land laws and in the way they are implemented. In the early 1980s, two-thirds of the agricultural workers in Peninsular Malaysia, and nearly all *padi* farmers, were Malays. An even higher proportion of agricultural workers is indigenous in Sarawak and Sabah.

Life in a Malay village devoted to rice cultivation has often, almost longingly, been described by Western observers as rustic, romantic, and tranquil. The setting depicted is one of serenity: small clusters of neatly maintained wooden houses on stilts surrounded by green fields of rice and symmetrical rows of irrigation canals, huge water buffalo patiently and ponderously pulling the plow or contentedly lying neck-high in muddy ponds. The mosque or the *surau* (a religious building that does not have the status of a mosque) emits rhythmic calls to the Islamic faithful, while the village coffee shop–cum–general store provides a locale in which villagers can mingle during leisure periods. The people in this scenario blend with the surroundings, constituting a polite and deferential society, ordered by rank, guided by patron-client relations, and imbued with a spirit of *gotong royong* (cooperation).

Here leisure time is culturally valued; ambition must not exceed village norms, and money, beyond family subsistence, is used for ceremonies or spread around to gain respect. The mood is one of acceptance and fatalism. Here Islam, itself containing strains of *Sufi* mysticism, has blended with traditional customs, some derived from Hinduism, which collectively constitute *adat*, a whole system of shared traditions, values, and beliefs. Nature spirits and "ghosts" still abound and must be placated through prescribed ceremonies and occasionally with the help of the *bomoh* (medicine man).

Islamic ritual obligations are central to village life. The mosque or *surau* functionaries call the faithful to prayer five times a day. Most villagers are unable to attend that often, but obligations can be satisfied by setting down a small prayer mat anywhere and, while facing Mecca, silently reciting passages from the Quran and prostrating oneself on the mat. Friday is the Islamic holy day. Friday prayers at the mosque, where the sexes are segregated, represent the major religious and social event of the week. Ritual cleansing and the readings from and interpretations of the Quran (the "sermon") are the top priority, but the gathering also provides opportunities for the exchange of information on weddings, engagements, funerals, feasts, Ramadan (fasting month) preparations, and the like; moreover, problems, such as the arrangement of irrigation schedules, can be discussed and perhaps solved the "Malay way" through consultation and consensus. In several of Malaysia's states, Thursday and Friday constitute the weekend.

However, this attractive picture, fringed by waving coconut palms, conceals reality in two important respects. It does not convey the effects of modernization, which range all the way from improved transportation, the availability of television, and the wearing of T-shirts at elections, to such misdirected efforts as the purchase of refrigerators that rust away, unconnected to electricity, and the use of toilets as flower vases. Such a picture also hides the reality of a pervasive rural poverty that primarily affects the Malays. This is not to overlook the plight of many poor Chinese and Indians who work on the land. A particularly scandalous example, revealed in 1983, concerned about thirty Indian estate workers who had been ill-treated as well as cheated of their wages. Statistically, however, more Malays have suffered. In spite of heavy government outlays on irrigation, which made double-cropping of rice possible, and on support services, an official 1982 survey found that poverty among *padi* farmers was as high as 76 percent. A poverty line had been worked out and was adjusted annually; below it, minimal needs for food, clothing, shelter, transportation, fuel, and power could not be met. The poverty rate for all of Peninsular Malaysia was about 43 percent.

Rural poverty could have social and political, as well as economic, implications. Economically, the major problem is one of unequal land distribution, which results in cumulatively unequal rewards. The "green revolution" has led to a situation in which the rich and middle-income peasants with sufficient land have been able to afford the much higher production costs involved in the new technology (such as expenditures on machinery and fertilizer), thus enabling them to improve their economic positions and to augment their holdings. The poor peasants, for the most part, have not been able to take advantage of these agricultural breakthroughs; consequently, their position is no better, and relatively it is worse. Among *padi* farmers 62 percent own less than 1 hectare, about 2.5 acres, the minimum size necessary to stay above the poverty line (about half the rubber smallholders own less than 1 hectare). The new technology has also eliminated many jobs formerly done by members of the poorer peasants' families, which used to bring in extra income. As a result, many small rice farmers are in debt, often to Chinese middlemen who have advanced credit to them.

There have been suggestions that the government should undertake land reform (e.g., by restricting the size of holdings or absentee ownership) or, conversely, that it should no longer subsidize uneconomic peasants but should force them off the land. Until recently, however, the government was unwilling to disturb a large and reliable political constituency, or to contribute to disruption that might politicize the peasantry along class lines. Its policy was to encourage a controlled "mental revolution" among the peasants, in the hopes that they would modernize their work habits and organize for cooperation through the medium of such groups as the farmers' association. It did not want them to abandon their attachment to the land and village life and customs. In spite of all these considerations, the government announced a drastic change in policy in 1984 (see the section on poverty in Chapter 6).

THE URBAN SETTING

In the 1970s and early 1980s, there has been a steady rate of growth of the urban population in Peninsular Malaysia, about 4.5 percent a year. This rate was faster than that for the population as a whole; hence the *proportion* of the population that was urban increased from 29 percent in 1970 to 37 percent in 1980. Ethnically, the increase has been faster for Malays; by 1980, 21 percent were urban compared with 15 percent in 1970.

Some qualifications are needed to fill out the picture. The figures just given understate the movements from rural to urban areas because they do not include people who moved to the outskirts of towns; these people are not classified as urban, although in most respects they lead an urban way of life. In addition, there were great variations in the physical distances moved. In some areas in the interior the nearest town is quite remote, even more so in Sabah and Sarawak than in Peninsular Malaysia. Moreover, people often did not move to the nearest large town. The northern states of Peninsular Malaysia registered movements of population not just from country to town but also to areas in other states that were growing faster economically—principally, the Kelang Valley in Selangor, the site of Malaysia's most rapid industrial expansion.

The four largest towns are Kuala Lumpur, George Town (Penang), Ipoh, and Johor Bahru, which together account for about 40 percent of the urban population. Kuala Lumpur, the largest, had almost a million people in 1980. The second two had about a third of a million each, and the last, about a quarter of a million.

The government did not set targets for urban growth in its New Economic Policy, which took effect in the early 1970s. Clearly, the policy implied that urbanization would increase because it provided for economic growth in nonagricultural sectors and for Malays to become more active in these sectors. Actually, however, the policy did not greatly increase the rate of urban growth, which had already been occurring in any case. Some politicians believed that the Malays would benefit from urbanization, not just because of better job opportunities but also because of the quicker tempo and greater sophistication of urban life. But as others saw the dangers of too rapid urbanization, the government took steps to locate some industrial projects, not in the major centers but in towns with populations between 40,000 and 75,000 or in newly created townships.

Urbanization also affected the areas *from* which populations moved. Given the prevalence of rural poverty, it might seem that urbanization could only help the rural areas by draining off surplus labor. But, on reflection, it is obvious that those who left were for the most part young and enterprising people. Thus the effect of their departure was often a shortage of labor; some fields had to be abandoned, while others had to be cultivated, rather ineffectually, by older people. The plight of such villages was well expressed in the title of a newspaper article: "Coping Without the Young Ones."[10] The paradox lay in the failure to use land effectively when good land was becoming scarce.

Town Life

Only a very impressionistic sketch of town life can be attempted here. The picture of village life given earlier, although a little idealistic, presents a decided contrast to life in the large towns, particularly in Kuala Lumpur, the capital city, which is taken here as an example. In Chinese areas, whether in overcrowded tenement blocks or shacks, the prevailing impression is one of a surplus of noise and smells. As J. M. Gullick described it, the inhabitants' range of occupations represented is varied, with self-employed workers, street hawkers, market peddlers, trishaw drivers, craftsmen, employees of small businesses, truck drivers, and so on.[11] The Malays are largely segmented, living in their own *kampungs*, which resemble real rural *kampungs* as closely as the conditions will permit. Many of the poor of both groups, as well as Indians and others, live in shacks in squatter settlements. About a quarter of the city's population consists of squatters, and about a third, including the squatters, have

The Kuala Lumpur Railway Station, sometimes described as an example of Victorian-Arabic architecture, was built by the British. This interesting building, reflecting the character of early Kuala Lumpur, is being preserved as a "national heritage building." (Courtesy of the Ministry of Information, Malaysia.)

inadequate housing. Kuala Lumpur, like Malaysia as a whole, fell behind schedule in planned house construction in 1981–1984. Linking the various sections of the city are concrete freeways with occasional traffic jams. The traffic is still not so congested as in Bangkok or Manila, for the city is much smaller and the quality of road construction is superior; however, the estimate that it will have nearly one car per household by the year 2000 is frightening. Two related mass transit systems are now being planned, which should be of some help. At any rate, the congestion in the city will soon be partially relieved by the transfer of some government departments to Janda Baik, some twenty miles away.

A draft master plan has been drawn up for Kuala Lumpur that entails substantial rebuilding. Early drafts of the plan earmarked the city center for urban renewal and the construction of high-rise apartments and condominiums, which would intensify traffic, parking problems, and pollution. In a decade or so, the high-rise would become the norm. To be sure, compared with most other Southeast Asian cities (including Melaka and George Town in Penang), Kuala Lumpur has no very old buildings and few historic or even graceful ones; yet it would be sad, indeed, if its identity and personality were destroyed.

Drafts of the plan have been criticized along ethnic lines. Whether the attempts to reduce the present ethnic segmentation will be effective is not yet known. But there have been Chinese complaints about the way in which Chinese business premises have been compulsorily acquired for demolition and about early drafts, later amended, that made provision for Muslim, but not for non-Muslim, cemeteries.

Such physical changes obviously affect the people concerned. Other effects stem from the transition from a rural to an urban environment. The physical appearance of a town may be familiar to new arrivals because of their exposure to films and television. But there can still be a psychological shock—one especially severe for Malays given the prominence of Western and non-Malay culture. They may react by stressing those aspects of their identity which provide them with support—for instance, religion, particularly the rigid and exclusive versions of it. On the other hand, non-Malays who live near Malay areas have to accustom themselves to hearing the Islamic call to prayer five times a day.

Western influence in the towns is inescapable and more marked than in the countryside. It can be seen in the modes of dress, notably jeans (thus requiring that the references to exotic local dress in Chapter 1 be qualified somewhat). It is also seen in the fashion for fast food (McDonalds, Kentucky Fried Chicken, A&W, etc.) and for video games. At higher levels of expenditure, it is evident in the popularity of "in" discotheques, such as the Tin Mine in the Kuala Lumpur Hilton. Less obviously, some Western practices that entail the adoption of "intermediate values" have become current, such as modern methods of birth control. Another complex instance of acceptance, in the face of seemingly strong initial barriers, has been Malay reconciliation of Islam and capitalism, as in the notion of the Islamic Bank.

Until recently, it was plausible to assume that the more highly educated Malaysians would adopt life-styles partly shaped by Western influences, which in turn would be imitated by others who were less well off. Nowadays, however, as far as Malays are concerned, contending with the acceptance of Western practices, which only a few years ago seemed natural and inevitable, is the countervailing force of the *dakwah* movement, to which Malays are attracted for the reasons mentioned above. Visually, this has produced extreme contrasts in women's dress, as well as less evident but more complex spiritual conflicts. Other changes have occurred as well since Husin Ali compared rural and urban areas; in the process, he noted that certain behaviors that would tend to be censured in the village, such as drinking alcohol openly, were not subject to effective sanctions in the towns.[12] Recently, for example, there has been strict enforcement of Malays' compliance with prohibitions against eating or drinking during the specified times in the fasting month.

The human side of urbanization needs to be stressed. In spite of the "protection" given by living in an area where there is a concentration of one's own ethnic group, the possibility of paying visits to one's former village, and the support of religion, the impact of city life may be traumatic. This may be especially so if employment is not available, or if the job obtained is ill-paid or entails irregular hours of work. These are the personal factors that planners' assessments of urbanization as "a way of bringing Malays into the labor force" totally fail to convey.

The Role of Women

An accurate recent summary of the role of women in Malaysia (one that needs only minor qualification) is "subordination right across the board."[13] To be sure, by the early 1980s, women made up more than a third of the labor force, but they were far less prominent in top positions than women in the Philippines and far less active in small business, especially trading, than women in Thailand. During the 1970s, the proportion of women in administrative and technical positions did not improve; it was only 0.2 percent as compared with 2 percent for men.

As a consequence of the tendency toward an "ethnic division of labor" in Malaysia, the occupations of Malay women differ from those of Chinese women. Traditionally, Malay women have been employed in agriculture, particularly in such jobs as weeding and planting. With the spread of technology and mechanization, the need for their services has declined, thus contributing to rural poverty. As a consequence, Malay women have migrated to the towns, particularly to the electronics industry, in which those between eighteen and thirty-five currently constitute 90 percent of the labor force. This outcome confirms the generalizations made earlier about the difficulties of adapting to an urban setting. Malay women have found it hard to conform to industrial discipline and have suffered from cultural and religious dislocation. Yet most prefer urban life, with all its problems, to their previous rural existence. By contrast, a smaller proportion of Chinese women are employed in factories. It is more usual for them to work in the numerous small Chinese family businesses.

In addition to the fact that a higher proportion of women than men are employed in subordinate positions, they are discriminated against by being paid less for equal work and in having less job security. Moreover, given the low proportion of women in administrative and technical positions, it is not remarkable that they lack prominence in the civil service, the judiciary, the press and other media, and interest groups. Politically, in 1984 there were only 8 out of 154 women in the Dewan Rakyat and only 6 women out of 61 ministers and deputy ministers. In accordance with the strength of UMNO within the government, Malay women were *relatively* more prominent in political positions than non-Malay women. Yet the women's wing of UMNO, Wanita UMNO, plays only a small role in deciding party policy, and at the local level UMNO women "participate" by attending party meetings and gatherings but provide minimal input.

Education statistics suggest that the position of women may yet improve. Although (1) the female illiteracy rate is double that for males, (2) slightly more men than women have a secondary education, and (3) twice as many men have a tertiary education, the gap is narrowing. In particular, more women in universities are now venturing into previously male fields, such as law, medicine, and engineering. Malay women, especially, have made great advances in education.

Nevertheless, among all ethnic groups, women have to contend with opposition supported by the weight of tradition. Although the disadvantages arising from Islamic law are being reduced for Malay women (e.g., by making divorce and polygamy harder for Malay men), the spread of *dakwah* makes advance more difficult. Few Malaysian women can say (as did a Malay woman cabinet minister) that there are no ascribed roles for her husband or herself in the house: "Whoever is free, my husband or I, takes out the dustbin, takes the kids to the clinic, washes the bathtub, or goes marketing."[14]

EDUCATION

The very direct link between culture and socialization and education, especially where the language of instruction is concerned, has made education an emotional and contentious issue in ethnically divided Malaysia.

Under the British there were several distinct tiers of education. The most prestigious consisted of the English-language primary and secondary schools, attended by the children of the Malay aristocracy and wealthy urban Chinese and Indians. Many Malays went on to the renowned Malay College at Kuala Kangsar en route to employment in the elite sector of the civil service (often via an overseas university). The University of Malaya was founded in 1949 and gradually displaced the Malay College in importance.

A second tier of education was the secular Malay-medium primary school system, which the British established and supported (they also reorganized and assisted the Malay-Arabic Quranic schools). The British, Malay aristocracy, and Malay peasants concurred that Malay education should be rudimentary, mainly for males (the peasants opposed sending their daughters to school), and designed to avoid alienating rural Malay youth from peasant life. There were no Malay-medium secondary schools.

The third tier was composed of the vernacular Chinese and Indian (Tamil) schools. The British encouraged the Chinese to establish, oversee, and finance their own primary and secondary schools. Beginning in 1924, for political reasons, some supervision over the curriculum and teacher recruitment was imposed, and small aid grants were initiated. Tamil primary school education was started on the rubber estates, which were required to provide facilities. There were no Tamil secondary schools.

Postindependence Education Policy

The trend since independence has increasingly been to impose a national Malay-medium education system on the country. In 1957, an ordinance was passed in which it was stated that a national system of education with a common syllabus would be established. In addition, Malay would be taught in all aided schools, Malay-medium secondary schools would be rapidly established, and all government exams would be in Malay and English only. This last point was controversial and led to some protests and disturbances, because it meant that Chinese and Tamil students could not take exams in their own vernacular. A new act in 1961 stated that after 1967 Malay should be the "main medium" of secondary education in aided schools, and it empowered the minister of education to convert schools to the Malay medium, thus raising Chinese and Tamil anxieties about the long-term future of their schools. Government assistance to Chinese secondary schools was terminated in 1962, so many converted (theoretically at least) to English to maintain aid.

After the May 1969 riots, the governing elite was determined that education would more fully reflect the intended Malay basis of society. The idea was not simply to promote cultural unity; it was also to provide the means for Malays to "catch up" in education and economic pursuits. In July

1969, the minister of education announced that henceforth government-aided English-medium schools would be replaced by Malay-medium schools, one year at a time from primary to university, beginning in 1970. Thus, by 1976 all peninsular English primary schools had been converted, and the process for secondary schools was completed by 1982. Moreover, almost all subjects at the university level are now taught in *Bahasa Malaysia*.

Accompanying this drive to help educate the Malays was the establishment of more universities; moreover, through quotas and scholarships, ethnicity was given priority over merit in university enrollment. Malay enrollment at tertiary institutions increased from about 20 percent in 1963–1964 to more than 65 percent in 1975.

The Chinese Education Backlash

The defense of Chinese education has been an emotional political issue among the Chinese, especially since 1969. It is viewed as important for the maintenance of Chinese culture and is seen in terms of ethnic loyalty. To some extent it symbolizes alienation. The defenders of Chinese education contend that its "essence" (e.g., socialization into Chinese culture) can never be captured in another setting. With the phasing out of English education, various Chinese groups successfully promoted the conversion of Chinese secondary schools to independent status (not government-aided but subject to some controls) to resist the conversion to Malay. The certificate from these schools is recognized by the Chinese business community, by Taiwan, and by some Western universities. Furthermore, there were record enrollments in Chinese primary schools in the 1970s (specifically, a 21 percent upsurge in 1971–1978). This trend has continued despite the fact that facilities and qualified staff are lacking; indeed, the DAP in 1984 accused the government of ignoring the needs of Chinese primary schools in order to lower their effectiveness preparatory to converting them. Another decade-long Chinese effort was directed to the establishment of an independently financed Chinese-medium Merdeka University. This effort was finally defeated when the Malaysian High Court ruled in late 1981 that it was "not expedient" in the national interest, and a subsequent appeal was rejected.

In sharp contrast, Tamil primary education is in a very poor condition and is not being vigorously defended. Tamil school facilities are deficient, with a shortage of teachers, high dropout rates, low achievement levels, and declining enrollments (from 16,000 in 1967 to 13,000 in 1982). The Malaysian Indian Congress (MIC) is naturally reluctant to speak out against Tamil education, but it has asked that tiny estate schools (53 percent having fewer than 100 students) be replaced by "nucleated" area schools, where facilities and standards might be better.

Current Educational Trends

There are three major discernible trends in education: (1) an emphasis on basic skills through the "3R" program, (2) an effort to instill Islamic values or moral education, and (3) the imposition of controls on sponsored overseas education.

The 3R scheme (i.e., the new primary school curriculum) was launched in 1982 as a product of an earlier cabinet commission headed by Dr. Mahathir when he was minister of education, and followed up by Datuk Musa when he assumed the portfolio. The commission had decided that the problem with education was rote learning and overemphasis on exams while basic skills (the 3Rs of reading, writing, and arithmetic) and the inculcation of moral and ethical values were underemphasized. Generally, the program called for a modern approach (through play acting, music, art, dance, etc.) to the learning of basic skills. Initially, the program was criticized on the grounds that it intended to undermine Chinese and Tamil education, inasmuch as the syllabi were in *Bahasa Malaysia* and stressed Malay cultural themes (later, following MCA objections, the syllabi were translated for use in the vernacular schools). Now, after two years, the criticism comes mainly from certain teachers who complain that they are being treated as "overworked zombies." According to reports from the minister of education, however, surveys show that the program is widely accepted and that the students in it are performing above the average of students not in the program.

The second major trend concerns the instilling of Islamic values or moral education. Islamic studies have been increased from 30 to 150 minutes per week in national primary schools; girls are allowed to wear headscarves and boys long pants (shorts have been the traditional dress for school boys) in line with Islamic dress standards (female teachers in Perak have been issued strict dress codes, which are somewhat resented); more *Jawi* (Arabic script) is being taught; and more teachers are being sent to religious secondary schools. The alternative to Islamic studies for non-Muslims is an exam course on moral education. But some confusion exists as to its content and whether its basis is to be theological or ethical and philosophical. Finally, in line with the current Islamization program, the government has established an International Islamic University (IIU).

The third major trend in education is the government decision to send fewer of the younger students to overseas universities (and then only after a one-year orientation course) and to cease sending sponsored students for A-levels (college-preparatory classes) abroad. Not only has this program been expensive (about M$420 million in 1983), but some of the students have been engaging in antigovernment activities of an Islamic extremist variety. Students deemed to be misbehaving in this way may have their scholarships withdrawn. The government has reassured the non-Malays that this decision will not adversely affect their enrollment prospects in local universities. Moreover, in 1984 a sixth university was established in Kedah to ease the enrollment pressure. Arrangements were made in 1985 with some U.S. universities for Malaysian students to take the first two years of their degree courses in Malaysia and then transfer to the United States for the remainder of the course. The scheme is to be extended to other countries, and should enable Malaysia to make appreciable savings in foreign exchange.

The overall education picture is that a Malay national education system is in place, despite the continued (though difficult) existence of Chinese and Tamil education, and the emphasis is moving toward a government-controlled and coordinated "Islamization" of education.

THE MASS MEDIA

Government in Malaysia plays a much larger part in controlling the mass media than it does in most Western countries. Apart from any dangers of subversion, it is imperative that the media should not be used to inflame ethnic feelings. This, however, is not the complete explanation. The Malaysian government, like that in many other developing countries, wishes to inculcate interethnic harmony as well as certain moral values. The problem is this: Given these requirements, how much news and entertainment can be provided for the public?

The Press

Nearly all Peninsular Malaysians who are literate (over three-quarters of the population) read newspapers at one time or another. In 1983, the daily readership of Malay newspapers was about 2.5 million, compared with 1.5 million for newspapers in Chinese and 800,000 for those in English. Readership of the Malay papers was the fastest growing.

The most obvious government restriction is the requirement that every newspaper must have an annual license, a provision dating from colonial times. In addition, the government may give warnings or convey advice informally; to which newspaper editors naturally pay great attention. In 1973, the government requested a "blackout" of news about the MCA's internal difficulties, and a similar blackout occurred in 1983 concerning the constitutional crisis over the position of the king and the rulers. Two political veterans, Tunku Abdul Rahman, the first prime minister, and Tan Sri Dr. Tan Chee Khoon, former leader of an opposition party, share the distinction of breaking many silences on important issues in their columns in *The Star* newspaper. Sometimes a minister will criticize certain trends in newspapers in a public forum, as did the prime minister in 1984, when he deplored the tendency of *Bahasa Malaysia* newspapers to emphasize tales of horror and the supernatural, thereby provoking fear and hysteria, which in turn contributed to backwardness among the Malays.

Another possible means of control was created when the government news agency, Bernama, was made the sole distributor of news from all foreign news agencies in 1984, although, in response to criticism, the government denied that the intention was to censor news. In the same year the law was changed to make the importation and distribution of foreign publications more difficult.

Radio and Television

Radio and television programs are available throughout the greater part of Malaysia. Nearly three-quarters of all households own radio sets, and about half own television sets. Until 1984, these media were run by the government, which provides a number of domestic networks on both radio and television as well as an overseas radio service. Since independence there has been a conscious attempt to make use of these media to explain, and enlist support for, government policies. Radio and television have served to transmit the message of Islam (but from 1983 on they no longer conveyed the clamor of rock). They have also aimed to prevent any particular channel from presenting programs exclusively in one language, and in 1984 they stated that programs would be gradually restructured with a "balanced" (multiracial) audience in mind. It appears, therefore, that their policy is to provide programs in English, Chinese, and Tamil for some time to come, but increasingly to concentrate on Malay.

June 1984 saw the inauguration of a private television station, TV3, which at first was limited to viewers in the Kuala Lumpur area. Its establishment resulted partly from the government's new policy of privatization (see Chapter 6) but was also intended to compete with videotapes, which by then were widely available and attractive to those viewers who wished to have programs in the language of their choice and without moral or cultural "messages." Although the government gave up management, it has not relinquished control. TV3's programs are subject to regulation for conformity with the principles of Islam and the needs of national security. It is likely that additional private commercial television, as well as radio, will soon be available.

INTEREST GROUPS

In Western countries, interest groups do not exactly make life easier for governments but at least they are respected. In Malaysia and other neighboring Southeast Asian countries, neither are they such a "nuisance" nor are they accorded much respect. A few are actually sponsored by the government, as are some youth, farmers', and religious groups in Malaysia. The remainder, though they exert some influence, tend to be dominated by the government; they are tolerated but will be checked if they try to go beyond certain limits. Government attitudes are exemplified by the Societies Act, which was originally designed to register and control secret societies and subversive groups but was amended in 1981 to "smoke out" groups that the government believed were acting politically (though ostensibly formed for other purposes). ABIM, Aliran (a nonpartisan, multiethnic reform movement led by Dr. Chandra Muzaffar), and other organizations fought the amendments and secured some modifications.

Trade unions are an important group, although they are surprisingly weak for a number of reasons: the small size of business establishments, the individualism of Chinese workers, and, above all, government discouragement. In 1983, fewer than 20 percent of the labor force were union members. The largest single union is the National Union of Plantation Workers, most of whose members are Indian. Government toughness toward the unions was evident when the Airline Employees Union took illegal work-to-rule action in 1979. The union was deregistered, and the law was tightened so that unions can currently negotiate on conditions of service but not on wages. A recent trend toward in-house unions has occurred (with membership restricted to workers in a particular firm)—a trend based on the Japanese example but deplored by many union leaders. The unions are multiethnic, although Indians are disproportionately represented.

About 70 percent of the societies that have been registered are confined to one ethnic group—notably, the chambers of commerce (which, however, have a multiethnic "umbrella" organization on top) and the schoolteachers' associations. Other groups have links with a political party (e.g., the Chinese Chambers of Commerce have informal connections with the MCA).

Government has also acted to control university student bodies. Following the demonstrations by students subsequent to the 1974 elections and the students' marches supporting dissatisfied peasants in Baling (Kedah), the government reacted by passing the Universities and University Colleges Act of 1975, which prohibited students from supporting or becoming members of parties, trade unions, or other bodies without university approval.

Finally, not only is the power of interest groups considerably restricted, but their role in the process of passing legislation is also minimal. They have few opportunities to state their views on proposed laws through consultation. It is only after a law has been passed that the groups can agitate for amendments, or at least for favorable implementation. A good example of the latter was the Industrial Coordination Act of 1975, which was drafted in rather vague terms (see Chapter 6).

In sum, the leading themes running through this chapter concern the ubiquitous role of ethnicity, which every government policy has to take into account; the persistence of rural poverty; the consequences of migration from country to town; the dominant power of government as contrasted with the relative weakness of private groups; and the government's commitment to the task of reshaping the social structure through education and even to the extent of planning to promote a dramatic increase in population over the next century.

5
Political Institutions
and Processes

To understand Malaysian politics one must begin by recognizing that the most salient political division in Malaysia has been, and remains, that between the Malays and the non-Malays.

Under the British the status of the Malays was protected as that of the "indigenous race." When this status was threatened in 1946, the Malays united solidly behind a single political organization, UMNO, to fight against the "racial extinction" they believed the Malayan Union scheme represented. Since the time of their successful campaign, the major premise in Malaysian politics has been Malay political dominance or hegemony. Until the 1969 watershed, and in the face of the perceived threat of being overwhelmed politically in their native land by the "immigrant races," the Malays have insisted on political control and have remained acutely sensitive to the requirement of Malay unity.

Initially, however, because the British required it as a condition for independence and since then because the non-Malays are too large a minority to ignore, the Malays have not seized complete political control. Instead, a process of elite ethnic accommodation through the ruling multiethnic coalition party (the Alliance and its successor, the Barisan Nasional) has taken place. Every cabinet has been multiethnic in its composition.

Malay political dominance was understood by the political elite to be part of the "rules of the game," but this fact was disguised somewhat by ambiguity and the fiction of an equal partnership. The May 1969 riots and the subsequent emergency rule destroyed the fiction, ended the ambiguity, and also undermined some of the very real accommodation that had been achieved. From that point on, the Malays have made it abundantly clear that while they want non-Malay participation in government and will listen to non-Malay grievances, they are in charge and intend to remain so. They remain sensitive to "political encroachments" and the need for unity, but in the last decade the Malays have become less defensive and more confident. This new mood was reflected in the statement made by the prime minister to Muslims at the end of the fasting month on June 30, 1984: "In fact, we [the Malays] hold the reins of power and can generally determine our own future."[15]

In the following three sections of this chapter, we will examine the constitution and the role of formal institutions, the operation of the party system and elections, and styles and techniques of governing.

THE CONSTITUTION: FORMAL INSTITUTIONS

Like other constitutions, the federal constitution in Malaysia describes the powers of the various organs of government, their relation to each other, and the rights of the citizens. In addition, because the country is a federation, the constitution lists the respective powers of the federal and state governments. Unlike the U.S. Constitution, however, the idea is not to establish a system of checks and balances among the legislature, the executive, and the judiciary. Instead, power is concentrated in the prime minister and the cabinet, except that elections for the Dewan Rakyat (House of Representatives) must be held at least every five years, thus giving the electors the chance to change the party in power. There are three main keys to understanding the nature of executive supremacy. First, although the system of government is sometimes termed a "parliamentary" democracy, in fact the system operates in such a way that the leaders of the majority party in Parliament, through the exercise of party discipline, are in control of the members of the legislature. Second, in comparison to the United States, the role of the courts is much reduced. To be sure, the courts may declare a law unconstitutional when it conflicts with the constitution. But the governing party can *change* the constitution with relative ease; in many cases, the only requirement is a two-thirds majority of the members of each house of the legislature. The Malaysian Constitution must surely be one of the most amended constitutions in the world—on the average, about one amendment each year since independence. (It has been amended much more often than the U.S. Constitution.) In a way, this fact demonstrates a certain respect for the constitution; it has not been merely ignored or discarded, as is the case in some Third World countries.

A good illustration of the power of the executive over both the legislature and the judiciary is its ability to declare a state of emergency under Section 150 of the constitution. This has been done four times, twice for excellent reasons, during *Konfrontasi* with Indonesia in 1964 and after the 1969 riots. However, the other two instances, in Sarawak in 1966 and Kelantan in 1977, were emergencies only in the sense that the government needed to solve party and constitutional difficulties in the two states concerned. Furthermore, in 1979, after the application of the 1969 emergency legislation had been judicially declared invalid from 1971 onward (when Parliament began to sit again), the government passed a bill retrospectively validating that legislation. In the same year, a constitutional amendment was passed to remove proclamations of this type from the jurisdiction of the courts.

The Agung (King)

The third key to understanding how power is exercised is that, for the most part, "executive power" belongs effectively to the prime minister and cabinet, not to the *yang dipertuan agung* (king). Confusion has arisen, however, because the constitution mentions that on most issues the king must act "on the advice" of the government. In Britain, this requirement greatly reduced the power of the monarch, but it took centuries

The former *agung* in the ceremonial attire of the king. This is the Sultan of Pahang, Sultan Haji Admad Shah Al-Musta'in Billah Ibni Al-Marhum Sultan Abu Bakar Ri' Ayatuddin Al-Muadzam Shah. (Courtesy of the Ministry of Information, Malaysia.)

of evolving tradition to establish it. In Malaysia, it was hard for an *agung* to accept such a limitation within a few decades. This ambiguity lay at the root of a constitutional dispute between the *agung* (and some other rulers) and the government in 1983. The constitution was changed so as to limit the power of the *agung* to block legislation proposed by the government, although in a way his position was strengthened because the amendments explicitly recognized his power to *delay* for a time the passage of such legislative proposals.

The *agung* does indeed have a symbolic role, which in itself may encourage national unity. But the requirement that he be elected by his fellow rulers at least every five years allows an individual only a short period in which to make a big impact. There are also possible constitutional situations in which the *agung* could influence the operation of government. If no party had a majority in the Dewan Rakyat, he could exercise some choice in naming a prime minister, although even then his nominee would have to be able to command the majority vote in that house. Because of the overwhelming strength of the Alliance/Barisan, such a situation has not yet arisen.

The Prime Minister and His Cabinet

Inside the cabinet, the prime minister (always a Malay) is dominant. It is the prime minister, with the power to hire and fire, who chooses the cabinet. He also controls the agenda of cabinet meetings, sums up and is responsible for coordinating cabinet decisions, speaks for the government as a whole at public meetings, on television, or on visits abroad, and represents the government in dealing with the *agung*. If a minister differs from the prime minister on a policy issue, he must either keep silent about it or resign. Dramatic resignations are rare, however. Most ministers exit as part of a general "reshuffle" of the cabinet. The cabinet speaks with a single voice (in public at least) and it acts collectively. In the cabinet, very few votes are taken and there is no known instance of a prime minister being outvoted. Challenges to the prime minister's position come principally from outside the cabinet, as did those challenges to the authority of Tunku Abdul Rahman in 1969–1970 and Datuk Hussein Onn in 1978. Nevertheless, it is difficult for a prime minister *not* to include some prominent party leaders in the cabinet, even if there are political differences between them. When Dr. Mahathir became prime minister in 1981, he appointed Tengku Razaleigh to the cabinet even though they did not see eye-to-eye. When he reshuffled the cabinet in 1984 he appointed Razaleigh again, although in a less important job. Tengku Razaleigh was the most important UMNO leader in Kelantan, where UMNO was only slightly stronger than PAS, and his support was too valuable to lose.

Other considerations are relevant to the prime minister's formation of the cabinet. His choice is restricted to members of Parliament, although the person appointed could be from the Dewan Negara (Senate) rather than from the Dewan Rakyat. This device was used when Tun Razak first appointed Dr. Mahathir to the cabinet at a time when he did not have a seat in the Dewan Rakyat. The prime minister also has to give consideration to the representation of various ethnic groups and different parties in the Barisan Nasional. In a cabinet of between twenty and twenty-five members, typically about two-thirds are Malay (practically all of whom are members of UMNO)—a proportion greater than that before 1971. There may also be one or two members from Sabah or Sarawak. A fifth or a quarter are likely to be Chinese, and there will be one, possibly two, Indians. With very few exceptions, all of these ministers are in charge of a department of government. Some appointments may be personal, in the sense that the choice is based not on the person's position in the party but on a close relationship with the prime minister; a good example is Dr. Mahathir's choice of Encik Daim Zainuddin, a prominent businessman, as finance minister in 1984.

In descending order of importance, the other government appointments consist of deputy ministers, parliamentary secretaries, and political secretaries (although participants in the last category do not have to be members of Parliament).

Prime ministers use these jobs partly to try out younger people for possible promotion to higher office.

Parliament

In systems of cabinet government, as opposed to presidential systems, legislatures are often weak and sometimes serve only as a "rubber stamp." Thus, the lower house of Parliament in Malaysia (the Dewan Rakyat) is weaker than the U.S. Congress, as might be expected; however, it is also weaker than its counterparts in, say, Britain or Canada. Some of the features contributing to this situation are as follows: (1) The bills introduced are the government's bills and they are seldom amended as a result of changes proposed by private members; (2) the committee system is hardly ever used; (3) bills are not printed and circulated long in advance of being debated; and (4) the time given for debate is short. Parliamentary questions, which have some effect on the government in Britain or Canada, make little difference in Malaysia, and the use of parliamentary committees is minimal. Party discipline is strong, and it is almost unheard of for members to vote against their leaders.

The upper house (Dewan Negara), which is partly appointed by the government and partly elected by the state assemblies (in each case for six years), carries even less weight, having only a delaying power. It does debate some issues more fully than the Dewan Rakyat, but it is useful, if at all, mainly as a source of patronage.

The Judiciary

The restricted role of the judiciary was mentioned earlier. The country has a hierarchical system of courts as well as an entirely separate set of religious courts in each state. Apart from issues of purely legal significance, the most important question is the degree to which the judiciary has been independent in the exercise of those powers it does possess. The top judges are in effect appointed by the prime minister, who "advises" the king. The judiciary has in fact acted with a considerable degree of independence. Occasionally a decision

A view of the Tower Block of Parliament. The buildings of Parliament were constructed in 1960 on a 40-acre site just outside downtown Kuala Lumpur. (Courtesy of the Ministry of Information, Malaysia.)

might seem to reflect the influence of ethnicity. A case in point was the 1982 court decision that confirmed the government's power in disallowing the establishment of a predominantly Chinese university (Merdeka University). Two Malay judges were in favor of the government, whereas the third (a Chinese judge) opposed it. However, there are numerous examples of court rulings in which the government lost: One involved financial transactions by the then opposition-controlled state of Kelantan, and others occurred in which Chinese opposition members of Parliament had been tried for sedition.

Linked with judicial independence was the provision that in some important cases, final appeal could be made to the Privy Council in London. This arrangement has been upheld by some as giving support to judicial independence, but it has been denounced by others as a relic of colonialism discarded by certain former British colonies. In 1978 appeals to the Privy Council in constitutional and criminal cases were abolished, and in 1983 first steps were taken to amend the constitution so as to do away with such appeals in civil cases.

The Civil Service

The civil service has the reputation of being among the most efficient and least corrupt in the region. This impression is probably an accurate one, although the Mahathir government's policy toward the civil service is based on the premise that it is oversized (in early 1984, 23 percent of the work force was in the "public service," broadly defined) and that its discipline and dedication still need to be improved. As in other countries, there have been some spectacular "foul-ups," many of them, curiously, concerned with road transportation. In the late 1970s, there were seemingly interminable problems in establishing a workable and acceptable policy on the wearing of motorcycle crash helmets and also a series of ineffectual official regulations for restricting the tinting of vehicle windshields so that they would not be unsafe because of reduced visibility.

Ethnically, the higher "divisions" of the federal civil service contain a percentage of non-Malays equal to, or higher than, their percentage in the whole population, although in the lowest division 90 percent or more of the officials are Malays. The situation is different, however, if we consider the small group of administrative officials in the service who carry the greatest weight in decision making—namely, the Malaysian Administrative and Diplomatic Service (MADS). This is the successor of the former Malayan Civil Service (MCS), which in colonial times consisted only of British and Malays. Even after independence the ratio of appointments was four Malays to one non-Malay, thus implementing Article 153 of the constitution on the protection of Malays.

The MADS is often referred to as an "elite." But what does this mean? To be sure, before independence a high proportion of the Malays in the former MCS were of royal or chiefly descent. But by the 1970s, the scholarships and loans available to Malays had boosted their upward mobility, so that increasing numbers of Malays in the MADS had fathers who were peasants or Malay schoolteachers. Nor is the MADS an elite in the sense that it governs the country, while the politicians are mere figureheads. In fact, individual politicians vary in the degree to which they are capable, and desirous, of controlling civil servants. But although the New Economic Policy was evolved with the help of civil servants, the drive behind the concept was supplied by others, notably Tun Razak. And today there can be no doubt that the policies of the Mahathir government are substantially those of the prime minister himself.

Federalism: Government in the States

It may seem strange that Malaysia is a federal state while Indonesia, with ten times the population and six times the area, is not. The explanation lies mainly in the existence of the individual Malay states and British support for them, apart from the aberration of the Malayan Union proposal. In actuality, apart from the rulers, Malaya was a unitary state because of its high degree of centralization; constitutionally, it was disguised as a federal state. When Malaysia was formed, conditions in Sabah and Sarawak were sufficiently different from those in the peninsula to warrant additional powers and to make federal relations with these states less centralized, although it took federal politicians some time to discover this. But in Peninsular Malaysia the only important function of the state governments is dealing with land. Federal power was also extended by the designation of the area around Kuala Lumpur and, later, the island of Labuan (Sabah) as "Federal Territory."

The constitutional head in the peninsular states, apart from Penang and Melaka, is, of course, the ruler. In these two, and in Sarawak and Sabah, the head is a governor, appointed for a limited term and without hereditary succession. Rulers have certain religious powers as heads of the Muslim religion in their states. But, as with the dispute about the king's powers at the federal level, there has been some doubt about the degree to which such rulers are obliged to accept "advice" and how far they actually rule. As indicated earlier, this was a complicating factor in the constitutional crisis of 1983–1984. Indeed, in some states a ruler has caused the position of the chief political figure in the state, the *menteri besar*, to become untenable, thus leading to his replacement.

The Conference of Rulers takes two main forms. In one, the rulers and the four governors, accompanied by their appropriate ministers, meet to discuss national policy with the *agung* and the prime minister. In the other, the rulers meet by themselves to discuss certain religious questions and issues of constitutional importance, such as the election of the *agung*. The consent of the Conference of Rulers is necessary for changes in the law on certain subjects, such as the rulers' own powers and Article 153, which deals with the special position of the Malays.

The state system of governmental structure roughly parallels that of the federal system. There is an executive council corresponding to the cabinet and a state Legislative Assembly, consisting of one house only, corresponding to Parliament. In the states that have rulers, the head of the executive council is called the *menteri besar*; in the other states, he is known as chief minister. The importance of these bodies is limited by the small number of state functions (except in Sabah and Sarawak) and by the limited resources of the states, which depend heavily on the federal government for finances. However, land allocations and timber concessions in the past have been used to build up political support and in some states have led to extensive corruption.

As the weight of federal power and central control have become more apparent, the status of *menteris* and chief ministers has correspondingly declined, except probably in Sabah and Sarawak. At one time the holders of these offices were reckoned to have a status roughly equal to that of a cabinet minister. In the usual sequence now, the individual, often a protégé of an important federal minister, is appointed at a relatively early age, and then, if successful in the job, is "promoted" to the position of cabinet minister.

Local government, in the sense of government by locally elected officials, no longer exists in Malaysia. Elections were suspended during *Konfrontasi* in 1965 and were never resumed, as councillors were then being appointed by state governments. A restructuring of councils followed in the mid-1970s. Many elected councils had been inefficient or corrupt, were torn by party politics, often on issues beyond the competence of the council, and suffered from a lack of local leadership. More important, local government lacked any tradition in the society, as was the case in many other developing countries. At the grass-roots level the system derives from tradition, although it has changed in its mode of operation. In Peninsular Malaysia there is a *penghulu* (an office in existence before the time of the British), who is headman for an area covering several villages and nowadays is a civil servant. The *ketua kampung*, headman at the village level, is now, in effect, also a government servant usually appointed by the district officer, although sometimes the nomination is recommended by the *menteri besar*. The *penghulu* and *ketua kampung*, in conjunction with the district officer and other officials, are concerned with the implementation of development programs that have some local input but are the responsibility of the federal government, thus once again illustrating the high degree of centralization in the country.

The Military

Books on the governments of developing countries often devote many pages to the role of the military, but for Malaysia this is quite unnecessary. The armed forces play no appreciable role in the economy, unlike the Indonesian armed forces. Malaysia's armed forces, moreover, are (1) overwhelmingly Malay, (2) nonpolitical, and (3) geared principally to the provision of security against internal Communist guerrillas. The navy and air force are relatively small. Their personnel are more technically skilled than army personnel, and they contain a higher proportion of non-Malays.

In 1981, approximately 75 percent of the officers and 85 percent of the rank-and-file in the armed forces were Malay, including all of the top positions. The non-Malay officers are concentrated mostly in technical units of the air force and navy. About 80 percent of the total military personnel is in the army. Of the army's infantry battalions, twenty-six constitute the Royal Malay Regiment, which is all Malay, while 10 are multiethnic but predominantly Malay.

There is no national conscription, and the government has rejected calls for national conscription from the non-Malay community as being too costly. Moreover, given ethnic tensions, UMNO leaders naturally want a conclusive Malay dominance in the armed forces. However, the exaggerated ethnic ratios are not entirely by design—military service is not historically and culturally esteemed by the Chinese.

The armed forces have steadfastly remained out of politics. Those top officers who were invited into the councils of government during the state of emergency following the May 1969 riots returned to their regular duties when the country resumed parliamentary rule in 1971. There are several reasons for the absence of political intervention: (1) the armed forces inherited the British "Sandhurst" tradition; (2) the dominant political and military elites are of the same race, they are quite often linked by family ties, and their beliefs are compatible; (3) the government has protected the Malays and effectively pursued economic development without any military prompting; the military's interests are attended to in terms of budgets, salaries, promotions, and honors lists (hence the military is also reasonably noncorrupt). Furthermore, Malaysia's substantial middle class is viewed theoretically as a deterrent against intervention. Although military personnel legally cannot be involved in business, there are many business opportunities for retired officers.

Until recently, the almost exclusive role of the military (along with certain police units) has been quite successful jungle counterinsurgency against Communist guerrillas (see Chapter 2). Now the emphasis has shifted somewhat to include more preparedness against the threat of external aggression (e.g., through tank training).

PARTIES AND ELECTIONS

The constitutional limit to the life of Parliament is five years. Elections in Malaysia have been held seven times between 1955 and 1982, even during the Emergency and *Konfrontasi*.

Parliamentary elections in Malaysia are more like referenda than contests to see which party or coalition will form the next government. The dominant coalition party has captured a parliamentary majority in every election, winning from a low of just over 63 percent of the seats in 1969 (with 48 percent of the popular vote) to over 85 percent in both 1978 and 1982 (with about 60 percent of the popular vote). The opposition has had no reasonable expectation of coming to power in any of these elections. Rather, it has aimed at preventing the government from attaining the symbolic two-thirds majority, which is nearly always a necessary step if the constitution is to be altered, and it has used the electoral occasions as opportunities to air particular grievances. As such, elections serve as a weathervane, and it has become increasingly important to the government that it not be seen as declining in popularity. In 1969, when the Alliance performed at its worst, some of the opposition held a "victory" parade, unfortunately a contributing factor to the May 13th riots. Malaysia uses a "first-past-the-post" electoral system (the candidate with the most votes in each constituency wins), as in the United States and Britain. This electoral system gives an advantage to large parties and also magnifies the difference between votes and seats won.

Malaysia, as a federation, also holds state-level elections, usually at the same time as parliamentary elections are held. the Alliance/Barisan Nasional has controlled most of the peninsular state governments most of the time, but more competition has generally been seen in some areas at that level. The opposition has come to power for varying lengths of time in four states, and uncertainty over which party would form the state government in Perak and Selangor in 1969 contributed to the high emotions that culminated in the riots. At present, there is only one opposition-held state government.

Although elections in Malaysia are clean and honest by most regional standards (e.g., in terms of voter registration, lack of voter harassment, secret balloting, and honest vote counting), the use of government facilities and especially the delineation of constituency boundaries are increasingly viewed as unfair. Although "rural weightage" is considered an acceptable practice in many countries,[16] in Malaysia the disparity in the number of electors in constituencies is sometimes excessive. Since a large majority of Malays are rural dwellers, this practice swells the voting power of the Malays (with 55 percent of the total population in the peninsula, 79 out of 104 constituencies had a Malay majority in 1982).

Another trend has involved the drawing of boundaries in the urban areas so as to increase the number of Malay majority constituencies. For example, in the redrawn 1984 constituency boundaries, the Malays had a majority in three of the six Federal Territory seats. In 1982, they held a majority in only one of the (then) five seats. The new delineations cannot be explained by minor demographic changes. The adjustment has apparently been made to ensure further Malay dominance. But it does not help the chances of UMNO's non-Malay partners to contest in "consolidated" constituencies with still higher percentages of non-Malay voters (the Malays in minority constituencies have been dependable supporters of the Barisan candidates). Likewise, the redrawn constituency boundaries intensify the state election battles between UMNO and PAS; in fact, it has even been suggested that in the future PAS may be able to make a strong bid for control of the traditionally Chinese-led state of Penang. There are few checks on such boundary delineations, inasmuch as the recommendations of the electoral boundary commissions are not final but have to be approved by Parliament (in effect, by the government).

Political Parties in Peninsular Malaysia

Just as the federal government has been controlled by the Alliance/Barisan Nasional, the coalition has been controlled by UMNO, which is the dominant party inside it. In fact, at nearly every election UMNO could probably win enough seats to form the government by itself. It has provided every prime minister and deputy prime minister and assigns itself the majority of cabinet portfolios (including all the important ones since 1971). It contests and wins the greatest number of seats (although in some Malay-majority constituencies it gives a few safe seats to its non-Malay coalition party leaders). Additionally, in the peninsular states, all but one of the chief ministers and *menteris besar* are from UMNO, and the party may assume control over Penang when Chief Minister Dr. Lim Chong Eu retires.

Parties in Peninsular Malaysia have a strong ethnic basis, and an ethnic rather than ideological appeal. Membership in the old Alliance parties (UMNO, MCA, MIC) was based exclusively on ethnic origins (Malay, Chinese, and Indian, respectively) although UMNO theoretically opened its doors a crack in 1978 when it altered its constitution to allow admittance of Muslims who were not Malays. Some of the peninsular parties incorporated into the larger successor Barisan coalition, such as Gerakan and the PPP, consider themselves to be multiethnic. In fact, both are Chinese-dominated, with some Indians as well as a token Malay membership. In the opposition, PAS is a Muslim-Malay party (with associate membership for other Muslims), and the DAP is a Chinese-dominated multiethnic party.

The Barisan Nasional (like the Alliance before it) is an unusual permanent coalition. It is registered as a political party, as are all of its component members. The partners maintain their own party organizations, elect their own leaders, finance their own activities, and generally conduct their own campaigns. They are linked into a coalition at the top by the chairman (always the UMNO president), an administrative secretary-general, and a Supreme Council bound by the rule of unanimity. In fact, the Council has no significant political function and meets only occasionally. Coalition differences are worked out in the cabinet or through informal elite consultation.

Such is the overwhelming dominance of UMNO that its triennial party elections are often called Malaysia's "real elections." In some ways these elections are more open and, hence, more fascinating than the general elections. A substantial amount of time, money, and effort is spent on the campaigns, especially in recent times. Personality, job performance, grass-roots support, patronage links, and policy orientation, as well as the prime minister's support (which is usually oblique but recently has been more direct), all affect a candidate's prospects. Factions are formed, but they are generally informal, unstable, and shifting. A follower will support his or her patron but perhaps not the patron's ally.

UMNO's president becomes the prime minister (or vice versa), and by tradition its deputy president becomes the deputy prime minister. This arrangement has thus far ensured a smooth succession. The party's five vice-presidents (with the exception of the one from Wanita UMNO, the women's wing) constitute the next echelon and generally act as an "inner cabinet." Also important are the twenty members elected and six members nominated to the UMNO Supreme Council. Usually all important government policies and actions are discussed by the Supreme Council and inner cabinet *before* they are presented to the coalition government cabinet (although there was an exception to this procedure in 1983).

In the past, owing to Malay deference to leaders, incumbents have only rarely and tentatively been challenged.
This situation has changed in the 1980s. The deputy president
was seriously, though unsuccessfully, challenged in 1984, and
three of the five vice-presidents were replaced (two of them,
for different reasons, did not compete). Following a wide-
open scramble, the Supreme Council also contained many
new faces in 1984. Successful competition for high party
positions is necessary for gaining choice government positions
and for getting into the "succession lineup."

There are now only two important opposition parties in
Peninsular Malaysia—namely, PAS and the DAP, which hold
diametrically opposing views (PAS wants a Malay Islamic
state whereas the mainly non-Malay DAP proposes political
and cultural equality). They cannot hope to come to power
in the foreseeable future (the DAP probably never will,
although it could do so, to a marginal degree, in the unlikely
event of being invited, and agreeing, to join the ruling
coalition). The opposition faces all the problems normally
associated with being permanently in the political wilderness
in a setting in which the government occupies the political
center: internal rifts accentuated by frustration, defections
(co-optation being an effective government strategy), lack of
funds and access to patronage, and a tendency toward rad-
icalization (now especially apparent in PAS). The opposition
is also hampered by legal restraints, as will be discussed later
in the chapter.

Parties and Elections in Sabah and Sarawak

Political competition is newer to the Borneo region of
Malaysia than the peninsula, and in some ways it deviates
from the pattern in Peninsular Malaysia. There is a less strict
ethnic base to parties, partly because the two states are
ethnically so varied, and partly because there are historic
regionally based divisions between some of the ethnic groups,
especially in Sarawak. Sabah is ruled by an opposition multiethnic party and Sarawak by a multiethnic coalition that
includes some ethnically mixed parties. However, while Sar-

awak has a Muslim chief minister who is identified with UMNO and the Malays, Sabah has a Kadazan Catholic chief minister with whom Kuala Lumpur is somewhat uncomfortable.

Another difference is that politics and party formations in Sabah and Sarawak have been more centered on personalities and patronage (indeed, the latter has been rather blatant). In addition, parties and coalitions have been less stable, thus creating a less predictable and more fluid political situation.

Partly because politics in the Borneo states are peripheral to Peninsular Malaysia and have never had an important effect on the outcome of federal elections, and partly because Sabah and Sarawak have more powers than the peninsular states, the tendency of the federal government has been to abstain from interfering much in their politics. The exceptions to this rule have occurred when Kuala Lumpur has faced intransigent or defiant pro–state's rights chief ministers who it felt were obstructing federal goals or policies. By a variety of strategies, these chief ministers have been removed.

State elections in Sabah and Sarawak have tended to give scope to a full range of dirty tricks and monetary incentives, and at times have been unpredictable. In Sabah, Tun Mustapha's party successfully outmaneuvered its rivals in 1967. Later, however, when Mustapha's government became an embarrassment as a result of corruption, mismanagement, and repression of the opposition, and even threatened secession, the federal government in 1976 engineered both its downfall and its replacement by a new multiethnic party. The unpredictability of Sabah elections was shown clearly in April 1985 when a newly registered party, the PBS, won a majority of seats and formed the government.

Politics and elections in Sarawak are more complex than those in Sabah. Initially there was more than one party for each of the major ethnic groups, although few of the parties were ethnically exclusive. The composition of the government coalition varied, and often one party of an ethnic group would be in the government and the other in the opposition. This pattern changed after 1969 with the advent of additional coalition agreements and the consolidation of two basically ethnic parties into one. After 1976, when there was no longer any major opposition, only the Ibans, the largest indigenous group, remained splintered into two parties. The situation was further complicated in 1983 by the creation of an exclusively Iban party, which was admitted into the ruling coalition following a state election. The situation among the Ibans remains unsettled, however, and the older, predominantly Iban but Chinese-led party, SNAP, may either disintegrate or return again to the opposition.

In sum, politics in the Borneo states still remain more fluid and unpredictable than those in the longer-established system of Peninsular Malaysia.

THE POLITICAL PROCESS

As noted earlier, the major premise of politics in Malaysia is that the Malays are politically hegemonic; in other words, they are in control. This fact is evidenced by UMNO's control of important cabinet portfolios and the positions of prime minister and deputy prime minister and by its prominence in Parliament. UMNO also provides all of the peninsular states' *menteris besar* and chief ministers except one. Malay dominance is further shown in the constitutional provisions making *Bahasa Malaysia* the sole official language and Islam the national religion and upholding the functions of the Malay rulers. Further still, this dominance is reflected in the civil service and armed forces ethnic ratios, in certain privileges guaranteed to Malays in the constitution, such as university enrollment and scholarship quotas, and in preferences given to Malays and other indigenous peoples through the NEP.

Despite this political hegemony, however, Malay rule is not absolute. Since the 1950s there has existed a principle of interethnic elite accommodation of communal differences and power-sharing; however, more genuine interethnic bargaining occurred before the May 1969 riots. Since that time, the political parameters have been more clearly spelled out; there are certain Malay goals that are non-negotiable, except in terms of how these are implemented.

Still, the spirit of accommodation continues. Through compromises the non-Malays have attained favorable adjustments to their share of NEP targets and to university enrollment quotas. In addition, Chinese politicians have been able to convince the top UMNO elites that prohibiting Chinese-medium primary schools would lead to the serious disaffection of their community.

Styles of Rule

Governments in Malaysia have borne the stamp of the ideas, actions, styles, and personalities of its four prime ministers.

Malaysia's first prime minister, Tunku Abdul Rahman, perceived his role and function as being those of a leader who could stand above ethnic dissension and who could arbitrate communal differences. His style of rule was casual and relaxed, and he delegated authority easily. He sought to settle problems at the top and in private, after which the government would present a united interethnic public front. His government placed a high priority on avoiding ethnic violence. Some have termed his rule as feudalistic—as the Malaysian version of *noblesse oblige*, with an emphasis on loyalty and honor. The Tunku was instrumental in successfully guiding the country through the precarious initial postindependence years when some critics believed the ethnic communities were too deeply divided to live together peacefully. By 1969, however, ethnic militancy was building up. Although the elite could agree to disagree, this was not the case for the person on the street or in the *kampung*. The lengthy and rancorous election campaign in May 1969 culminated in terrible ethnic violence and effectively ended the Tunku's rule, although he did not actually retire until September 1970.

The Tunku's successor, Tun Razak, had long been considered "pro-Malay" (a stance every UMNO leader since the Tunku has had to assume before acceding to the highest post). A methodical, bureaucratic workaholic, almost simultaneously daring in planning and yet cautious in execution, Tun Razak was the right man for his times. He was straightforward, rational, and modern in administrative matters—as, for example, when he instructed civil servants to use the telephone for priority requests instead of relying on the traditional slow method of typed letters in triplicate. Yet in his political approach inside UMNO, he followed the traditional "Malay way" in emphasizing a striving for consensus, an avoidance of direct confrontations, and a recourse to subtleties, indirection, and use of Malay folklore, often invoking analogies to animals, whether favored (the mousedeer) or dangerous (the dragon), to indicate his political preferences at, for example, UMNO party elections. As a national leader he was a skillful politician and coalition builder. He was able to assuage the worst fears of the non-Malays while still fulfilling the demands of the new generation of rising university-educated Malays who wanted more concrete action to help the Malays economically (e.g., through the NEP). The Tun also set about reducing "politicking" not just by amending the Sedition Act but also by enlarging participation in the government by bringing additional parties into the ruling coalition. His administration initiated radical changes; they were achieved with so much political finesse, however, that the full impact probably still has not been fully appreciated in Malaysia.

When Tun Razak died suddenly while in office in 1976, he was succeeded by Datuk (now Tun) Hussein Onn. In fragile health, somewhat remote, deliberate, and slow to take action, Tun Hussein gave the country a necessary breathing spell in which to reflect upon its course of action. But this is not to dismiss his contributions. He ably handled dissension in UMNO, including a Communist witchhunt and the arrest on corruption charges of Dato Harun; he continued efforts already in progress to force Tun Mustapha's resignation in Sabah and oversaw the admittance of two new Barisan member parties from the Borneo states; and he astutely deflected the most abrasive aspects of the Islamic resurgence then gathering force in Malaysia. He also set a markedly high standard of noncorruption and honesty in high office.

Tun Hussein's retirement in 1981 marked the end of an era. With his successor, Dr. Mahathir, a new generation came to power—a generation not royally connected, not British-educated, not from a wealthy family, not legally trained. Even golf, avidly played by the first three prime ministers, lost the prestige it had gained as the sport of prime ministers. (It was not just a sport, in fact; considerable informal but important consultation took place in the rough and on the greens, and non-Malay leaders had to master it well enough not to be excluded from valuable informal contact with prime ministers.)

Dr. Mahathir is a serious, impatient, resolute, and direct individual; he has labeled himself "abrasive" and is sometimes considered sensitive to criticism. His administration has been relentlessly action- and slogan-oriented in an effort to "jolt" or propel the country, and particularly the Malays, toward modernization through such policies as Look East; Malaysia, Inc.; privatization; and industrialization (heavy industry). Deputy Prime Minister Musa Hitam has labeled the approach as one of "shokkus" (the Japanese corruption of English for "shocks"). At the same time, Dr. Mahathir has also sought to reinforce moral values and discipline in society, partly to counter the negative Western influences that often seem to accompany modernization and perhaps also to compensate for the decline of Malay deference and tradition. He has urged the expression of these desired values in accordance with Islam.

Depoliticization

Since the May 1969 riots and emergency NOC rule, which lasted until 1971, administrations in Malaysia have stressed the need to keep "politicking" to a minimum so that energies can be devoted to the task of economic development. According to Tun Razak, Malaysia did not possess the societal preconditions necessary to make Westminster democracy function smoothly and stably.

In 1971 the constitution was amended and the Sedition Act tightened to prohibit the debate, even in Parliament and in the state assemblies, of certain ethnically sensitive issues (e.g., language, citizenship). Actually, these restrictions have

The prime minister of Malaysia, Datuk Seri Dr. Mahathir bin Mohamad. (Courtesy of the Malaysian High Commission, Ottawa, Canada.)

not been rigidly applied; so long as the principles of government policy are not contested, reasoned criticisms are permitted. At the same time, most key opposition parties were co-opted into the government coalition to defuse political competition (the major initial exceptions were the DAP and SNAP in Sarawak [until 1976]). PAS was in the Barisan until December 1977, when it left under pressure.

The government has additional means at its disposal to limit political competition, such as control of the mass media and societies (see Chapter 4) and use of the Internal Security Act (ISA), which provides for detention without trial (see Chapter 7). The government also exercises strict control over demonstrations and processions, and election campaign rallies continue to be banned. All of this adds up to a policy of "depoliticization," which maintains political participation, and the political temperature, at a low level.

The Opposition

Numerically, the elected opposition is weak, with the Barisan usually holding about 80 percent of the Dewan Rakyat seats. The tradition of a loyal and respected opposition has never taken root in Malaysia. The government, with few exceptions, has regarded the opposition as obstructionist at best. Not many in government seem to appreciate the possible value of the opposition as a "watchdog" or "escape valve," or the fact that it can facilitate policy feedback. One of the few opposition members of Parliament to win the government's respect was Tan Sri Dr. Tan Chee Khoon, known in Malaysia as "Mr. Opposition."

At times, the parliamentary opposition has seemed more intent on delaying proceedings, arguing, or embarrassing the government than on offering constructive criticism. Moreover, at elections the opposition has often adopted strident and abrasive positions. However, on many occasions, in Parliament and outside, the opposition has constructively pointed out flaws or ambiguities in bills or policies, has disclosed irregularities or suspected graft or corruption, or has articulated genuine communal grievances and apprehensions. In these respects, the opposition has served a proper and useful function.

The view of the opposition as obstructionist has colored parliamentary procedure and decorum. The government sometimes uses its parliamentary majority simply to authorize rapidly the actions already decided upon. At times the opposition finds that it lacks access to information, that documents are unavailable, and that there is inadequate time for questions. On one occasion in 1983, for example, the government cut off the opposition by walking out and leaving Parliament short of a quorum.

The government has also hindered the opposition electorally through its prohibitions on discussion of sensitive issues, by banning campaign rallies and monopolizing the mass media, and (for the non-Malay opposition) by realigning constituency boundaries each decade. The one area in which some individual opposition parliamentarians, such as the DAP's hard-working Encik Lee Lam Thye in Kuala Lumpur, are not hindered is that of constituency work, which the government evidently considers socially beneficial.

The working of the system is consequently somewhat different from what the formal constitution might suggest. There is more of an authoritarian, sometimes paternalistic, approach directed toward achieving stability, making things work, and providing a basis for economic development. The other side of the coin is a policy of depoliticization by which limits are placed on political participation.

6

The Economy

Compared with most other countries in the world, Malaysia is economically well off. Its per capita income is the highest in Southeast Asia apart from those of Singapore and Brunei, and its credit is good. The Institutional Investor's Country Credit Ratings (New York) recently ranked it number 20 out of 107 countries. Even in 1983, at a time of recession, foreign investment constituted about a quarter of all approved projects in Malaysia. Japan is now the largest direct investor, having drawn ahead of the United States and Singapore. The economy deserves attention partly because of the government's successful management of its natural resources. It also merits study because of its New Economic Policy (which took effect in the 1970s) and because of changes in the 1980s that included its "Look East Policy" (which took Japan and South Korea as models), its privatization policy, and its plans to concentrate manufacturing on heavy industry.

During the 1970s, per capita income rose from M$1,142 (US$371) to M$3,639 (US$1,639), corresponding to a GDP growth rate of nearly 8 percent a year. During the recession, growth slowed down, but to a lesser extent than in many other countries—that is, to about 6 percent a year, equivalent in 1983 to a per capita income of about M$4,400 (US$1,900). By that time, the annual rise in the consumer price index, which had never really threatened to get out of control, had fallen to approximately 4 percent. In 1984, growth was over 7 percent, and it will probably be 5 or 6 percent in 1985, which would bring per capita income up to about M$5,000 (US$2,000).

In spite of these achievements, the figures just listed are *averages*. They conceal the tragedy of the poverty of individuals, as well as the great differences among the states. Selangor and the Federal Territory may be classified as high income, whereas Kedah and Kelantan, and possibly also Perlis and Sarawak, are low income; the remainder qualify as middle income.

Because of the recession, many planned targets were not achieved. Originally, the government had tried to meet the recession through a countercyclical policy of increasing its expenditure and stepping up public investment to match a lag in private investment. This resulted in substantial deficits but the government put a brake on spending in 1982, and the 1983 budget made substantial cuts in defense and development expenditures and in projects planned but not yet contracted for. Public expenditure on consumption goods and investment combined was scheduled to fall from 41 percent to 38.5 percent between 1983 and 1984. However, the 1983 budget still provided for a deficit, though on a reduced scale. The projected size of the deficit for 1984 was about M$7 billion—that is, about 10 percent of national income. Targets for private investment have not been met. Some foreign investors have been deterred by the size of the deficit (and the increased debt burden). In late 1985, also, a number of local companies' shares weakened considerably.

PRODUCTION

Malaysia's GDP has several components, some common to all countries and thus not particularly distinctive: government services; provision of water, electricity, and other utilities; and the services provided by hotels, restaurants, and so on. The emphasis here, however, is principally on the production of goods, many of them exported, which are dependent on the use of natural resources found in Malaysia and/or on Malaysians' acquired skills. The three obvious categories are agriculture (including timber), minerals, and manufacturing.

The broad picture over the last quarter of a century includes the fact that the agricultural sector has declined while the manufacturing sector has prospered. The agricultural decline is striking. This sector produced 60 percent of the GDP in 1950 but only 20 percent in 1980, and it is projected to reach only 15 percent in 1990. Nowadays, although fewer than 10 percent of new jobs are in the agricultural sector, it still accounts for 40 percent of those in employment—a measure of its social and political importance as well as of its economic inefficiency.

To gain an insight into probable trends in production, however, we must break down the three sectors into their chief components, each of which, in turn, has a different degree of potential for success. In addition, influences on production that originate from the supply side should be distinguished from those that principally reflect demand from potential markets for a product.

In the agricultural sector, rice is unique because it is not an export crop. Potential for production was greatly boosted by irrigation schemes (available for two-thirds of the rice land by 1980), which made double cropping possible. But production is still hampered by holdings that are too small and by too much reliance on traditional methods, as described later in this chapter. Rubber production suffers from some of the same problems. Moreover, the government, while opposed to expanding the area planted with rubber, recognizes the need for increasing the number of high-yield clones and for research into new uses for rubber. Palm oil, on the other hand, is more efficiently produced; although its large-scale production was begun much later than that of rubber (in the 1960s), it has now replaced rubber as the major agricultural crop. In the past, timber products were exploited without much regard for conservation. A few years ago, it was estimated that in Peninsular Malaysia there would be a serious depletion of timber by the 1990s (and only a few years after that in well-endowed Sabah), unless measures were taken to limit production. Such a policy is now gradually being adopted, so timber production is due to decrease. Concurrently, demand for timber has also fallen. In another sector, included under

A view of symmetrically planted rubber trees on a rubber estate. In the foreground a worker can be seen tapping the bark of one of the trees for latex, out of which rubber is derived. (Courtesy of the Ministry of Information, Malaysia.)

the broad heading of "agriculture," overfishing is threatening to reduce future catches.

Among minerals, the extraction of tin is dropping because it is becoming progressively more costly, and new sources are hard to find. In the last few years, however, the discoveries of oil and, later, natural gas have boosted the minerals sector. At present rates of extraction, Malaysia's oil reserves will not be exhausted for about twenty-five years, and they may last longer if the search for new fields is successful. Natural gas reserves will be sufficient for at least thirty to fifty years' use. Hence in both of these sectors, there are subsectors in which production will soon be severely restricted by depletion. The inference is clear: Plans need to be made quickly for switching productive effort elsewhere.

The fastest growing of the three main sectors is manufacturing (with about an 11 percent growth rate even during the recession). The range inside this sector is very wide with respect to the amount of value added to the raw materials used. The government has recently declared that it is encouraging heavy industry. Its rationale is that this type of industry should be given priority even over other types that have already been successful (e.g., electronics) because it provides a "spillover" that will help to support the growth of other industries and thus contribute to the building up of an industrial base.

EXPORTS AND IMPORTS: THE BALANCE OF PAYMENTS

Worldwide forces that dictate the demand, and the prices, for Malaysia's exports are almost entirely beyond the government's control. Efforts to keep up the prices of rubber and tin, taken in conjunction with other producers, have not had much success so far. Export prices declined during the recession but are expected to rise as the world economy improves. Obviously variations will occur in the degree of recovery of different products. Conservation policies for items such as tin and oil will also tend to limit export receipts. Moreover, export revenues will be influenced by the rapidity with which Malaysian exporters adjust to changes in market preferences; their reactions may have been too slow as far as some timber products are concerned. Costs are also important; other things being equal, Malaysia finds it difficult to compete with cheaper labor costs in China, India, Indonesia, Thailand, and the Philippines.

The relative ranking of receipts from various exports has changed somewhat in the last few years. In 1983, the value of exports from agriculture (including forestry and fishing) amounted to a little over a third of the value of all exports. Mining, including oil, was responsible for just under a third, as were manufactures. Fast-growing exports of natural gas, classified in none of these categories, amounted to 3 percent of 1983 exports.

The relative ranking of receipts from various exports has altered over the last few years. In 1984 the value of exports from agriculture, including forestry and fishing, amounted to over one-third of the value of all exports; mining, including oil (which has become much more important recently), was responsible for about one-third; manufactures made up over one-quarter; and exports of natural gas, not listed in any of the above categories, are growing rapidly.

In the "agriculture" classification, 1984 export revenues were highest from palm oil, followed by timber and rubber. In the minerals category, the prospects for tin as an export have decreased over the years and are now stagnant at best. For the next two decades or so, oil will be a dominant component of exports. Receipts from manufacturing exports currently derive mainly from electrical machinery and appliances, textiles and clothing, and manufacturing equipment. Electrical machinery and appliances have constituted a really big success story in manufacturing, with a high percentage of the electronics component deriving from U.S.-based firms. The future, however, may be more difficult, given competition from countries with lower wage costs than Malaysia. Clothing and textiles also face an uncertain future because of protectionist barriers put up by industrialized countries and competition from rivals, particularly South Korea.

Malaysia imports not only a substantial amount of food and manufactured goods but also machinery, equipment, and some oil and lubricants. During the recession, the price of Malaysia's imports tended to increase relative to the price of exports. A particular make of auto, which fetched a price equivalent to 39,000 kilograms of rubber in 1978, exchanged for 52,000 kilograms in 1983. Services such as freight, insurance, and travel (for which Malaysia's payments exceed its receipts) also rose sharply in price. Consequently, the balance of payments on current account (covering exchanges of both goods and services), in which Malaysia had previously enjoyed a surplus, turned into a deficit in 1981–1983. To help correct this situation, the government exercised restraint in its spending, increased duties on some imported food, took steps to achieve greater self-sufficiency in shipping and insurance services, and started a drive to attract more tourists. In July 1984, the then finance minister, Tengku Razaleigh, identified the balance of payments deficit as the "number one priority in the field of economic management." In 1984, the balance of trade (in goods) improved substantially, but the balance-of-payments deficit still constituted a major problem.

Japan is Malaysia's most important trading partner, accounting for almost a quarter of its total trade (Singapore and the United States are the next most important). Typically, Japan exports a higher value of goods to Malaysia than it imports and has a surplus in payments for services.

THE NEW ECONOMIC POLICY

These data provide a profile of the Malaysian economy, but to understand its present structure and future directions we must also take into account the social and political factors that shape government policy.

Origins and Objectives of the New Economic Policy

After independence was gained in 1957, while political power lay in the hands of the Malays, economic power, apart from the substantial share possessed by foreign business, belonged mostly to the non-Malays, especially the Chinese. The Bargain between the main ethnic groups that formed the basis of the 1957 constitution seemed to embody an ethnic distribution of power.

Even in the years just after independence, however, the government took some steps to improve the economic condition of the Malays. Apart from abstract considerations of justice or equity, measures to help the Malays, who lived mostly in rural areas and were relatively poor, were necessary if UMNO was to retain the bulk of its electoral support. An intensive program of rural development was launched, and personally supervised, by Tun Razak, the deputy prime minister, complete with "operations rooms" based on the military system used during the Emergency. An important instrument of development, though also a costly one, was the Federal Land Development Authority (FLDA, later FELDA), which cleared stretches of land, placed settlers on sections of it, and assisted them financially and with advice until sales of their crops enabled them to pay off their obligations and become owners. Another body, set up in 1950, was reorganized in 1965 with the rather grand title of MARA (Majlis Amanah Raayat, or Council of Trust for the Indigenous People). Its functions, which were more diverse and less uniformly successful than those of FELDA, extended to helping small business as well as agriculture.

During the 1960s, there were signs that government leaders and some other prominent Malays did not regard the Bargain as static. Apart from the use of MARA and other organizations, there was a greater emphasis on the utilization of Article 153 of the constitution (which concerned the "protection" of the Malays) to provide them with more business licenses, scholarships, and so on. Malays also gained through improvements in rural education and by moving to the towns where economic opportunities were better. The big policy shift, however, occurred after the riots of May 1969. The Malay leaders were shaken and arrived at two significant conclusions. The ethnic violence, they believed, indicated the existence of economic grievances that called for drastic action. In addition, the diagnosis and appropriate remedies needed to be spelled out plainly. Ambiguities were no longer to be tolerated; the solution to ethnic conflict was not to "sweep it under the carpet" (to use a favorite phrase of Tun Razak) but to deal with it realistically and in the open.

The result was a "New Economic Policy" (NEP), which took shape in the early 1970s and was embodied in a series of five-year plans. Targets were set, mostly up to the year 1990, coinciding with the end of the fifth plan. The 1971–1975 plan (actually the "Second Malaysian Plan," because the first one was currently in operation) explained the new approach. The objective was national unity, which could be attained only through greater equity and balance among social and ethnic groups, and only if poverty were reduced and adequate employment opportunities were provided. Consequently, the NEP had two "prongs." The first involved the reduction, and later the eradication, of poverty as well as the restructuring of society to correct economic imbalance, thereby reducing and eventually eliminating "identification of race with economic function." The second prong was to include the modernization of rural life and the creation of a Malay commercial and industrial community at all levels.

The Malays (and other indigenous peoples) would benefit under the first prong inasmuch as a high proportion of them were poor, as compared with Chinese or Indians. Under the second, they would gain through entering the world of business, where the rewards were greater than those in agriculture. The NEP did not aim at growth per se as, otherwise, free enterprise would have been encouraged irrespective of which ethnic group would benefit. As it was, a Chinese politician remarked that "the government is trying to turn Malays, who are not good at business, into entrepreneurs, while it puts limits on the Chinese who *are* good at it." This comment was only partly relevant, however, because the New Economic Policy was not just what the name implied but also a new *political* policy. Yet, in another important way, growth was indispensable to the policy's success, because the policy was founded on the premise that the economy would expand so rapidly that groups other than the Malays would not suffer but would also actually gain. Without growth, on the other hand, a zero-sum situation would arise, and ethnic tensions would become much more likely.

NEP objectives may be classified as follows: to attack poverty; to attain an "ethnic balance" in various economic sectors and occupations; to create more Malay entrepreneurs and managers; to raise the share of capital held by Malays; and to increase the proportion of Malays attending universities and similar institutions.

134   THE ECONOMY

Poverty

The reduction of poverty has proved to be the most intractable target. In the early days of the NEP, data were lacking on the incidence and severity of poverty among different sections of the population. However, for the third and fourth plans, beginning in 1976 and 1981, respectively, the government, by then in possession of better information, stepped up the resources devoted to fighting poverty. The incidence of poverty in Peninsular Malaysia (see Chapter 4) was targeted to decline from about 49 percent in 1970 to about 17 percent in 1990. Early government reports were quite optimistic about the results. But progress was slower than expected in the rural areas, where the great majority of the poor live, although there were gains in the spread of services and improvements in the quality of life, as shown by the increased provision of water, electricity, health, and education; the decline in infant mortality rates; and so on. In particular, the Malaysian social security system had been successful in making medical care available for almost all Malaysians.

Although the incidence of poverty fell from 1970 to 1980, it had apparently risen again by 1983. As explained in Chapter 4, poverty was greatest among the Malays, particularly those in agricultural occupations. Poverty had also increased among some non-Malay groups, such as estate workers (mostly Indians). In Sabah and Sarawak as a whole, poverty is currently declining, but some indigenous groups, notably the *Bidayuhs* (Land Dayaks) in Sarawak, are much poorer than the average. The Malay rate of unemployment is also higher than that for non-Malays, although the rate for the indigenous peoples in Sabah and Sarawak is higher still.

Accordingly, in spite of improved facilities in rural areas and the drive to modernize agriculture, it appears that the campaign against poverty has not been very effective. Kedah, which received huge investments in irrigation and large subsidies, was the poorest state of Peninsular Malaysia in 1983. In fact, many government payments do not entail a substantial transfer of income to poor Malays. Much of the expenditure benefits local contractors, many of whom are non-Malays, as well as multinational firms, which gain from the more extensive use of machinery, fertilizer, and so on.

The poorest Malays do not always get the most help from the government. Calculations for the early 1970s showed that the average Malay student in a postsecondary institution, whose potential earnings were high, received a larger subsidy than the average Malay farmer.

As suggested in Chapter 4, the size of many rice and rubber smallholdings is simply too small to be economic. By 1983, the government had recognized this fact; in 1984, it announced that it would take a number of measures, some constituting a "New Agricultural Policy," to make more efficient use of resources. The prime minister had decided on a bold switch from previous policies designed to keep the farmers on the farms. Given the government's new emphasis on industrialization, those policies were no longer appropriate. A central element in the new policy was that small rubber, rice, and other holdings would be regrouped into larger and more economic units, thus facilitating mechanization, and that these estates would be developed cooperatively, although the owners would retain the titles. *Kampungs* would be restructured to reduce infrastructure costs, and new marketing facilities would be provided. On the other hand, farmers would not be *forced* into "rural urbanization," so the process of amalgamation would obviously require careful handling. Given the existing state of financial stringency, and in accordance with the concept of privatization, future farm and estate development would have to depend largely on private funds. At the same time, 1984 changes in the land code prevented further fragmentation of land. In addition, as a reflection of the free market approach, some agricultural subsidies were reduced.

A bold agricultural policy was evidently needed. The main reservation expressed was that the returns to an individual peasant after amalgamation would be based on his or her original holding. So the scheme would perpetuate much of the inequality between those who had started with large holdings and those who initially had only small ones.

Moreover, opportunities for additional employment on the new estates would have to be produced by the government in order to supplement income.

The government has shown more concern about poverty than about the related issue of the unequal distribution of income. It has been suggested that under the NEP, income has become less equally distributed among Malays, thus leading to the creation of a small Malay capitalist class. Firm evidence is lacking, although one can identify a relatively small group of Malay directors who own a high proportion of the total shares owned by individual Malays, just as one might also discern the existence of a quite small number of rich peasants. Obviously, there is a good deal of conspicuous consumption by Malays; gone are the days when a Malay driving an expensive car in Kuala Lumpur was almost certain to be a chauffeur. The view of the prime minister is that some disparity of incomes among Malays is inevitable and, indeed, that it indicates the success of the NEP in producing viable Malay businessmen. The prime minister believes that to try to remove disparity by bringing down the wealthy rather than by raising the poor would damage incentives and economic growth.[17]

Achieving Balance in Employment

The NEP was also meant to ensure that employment in various economic sectors, and at various occupational levels in these sectors, should reflect the racial composition of the country. Malays, for instance, had been overrepresented in agriculture and underrepresented in manufacturing, commerce, mining, and construction, as well as in administrative and managerial positions and in professions such as medicine, engineering, and accountancy. Thus, they were concentrated in occupations with incomes below the general average. On the other hand, non-Malays were underrepresented in agriculture. Targets were therefore set for various sectors of the economy in order to correct this "imbalance." To achieve these targets, Malays had to be trained, either in universities or similar institutions, or through short courses given by bodies such as MARA. In addition, private firms had to be willing to employ Malays. This policy was enforced by the Industrial Coordination Act (ICA) of 1975, by which businesses (with the exception of small ones) had to employ certain percentages of Malays. By the early 1980s, these targets were being met—for instance, with respect to professional and technical workers. From 1970 to 1982, the proportion of Malay doctors had more than tripled, and there were two and a half times as many Malay engineers. At managerial levels, however, Malays were still poorly represented.

Malays as Entrepreneurs and Managers

A great deal has been written about the problems of turning Malays into entrepreneurs. The colonial myth of the "lazy native" has been countered by citations of Malay traders who flourished at the peak of the Melaka Sultanate five hundred years ago. During the colonial period, most of the business not in the hands of the colonialists and other Westerners was carried on by non-Malays, mostly Chinese. It was easy to persuade urban Malays that business was a good thing and that profits were desirable, but without government help the obstacles to success were formidable. The environment was alien; in an effort to make contacts with wholesalers or to obtain franchises, for example, the Malay would-be entrepreneur would be faced with a closely knit Chinese business community. Credit would be hard to get because financial institutions were aware of few Malay business successes but of quite a few Malay business failures. The government did provide business training; it also ensured that credit was made available. The former objective was accomplished through such organizations as MARA, the MARA Institute of Technology (ITM), and the National Productivity Centre; the latter was achieved by MARA and by banks, backed up by government guarantees. But this was not the end of the story. An official in one of the advisory organizations said that clients "need more than just telling and showing. They need a whole gamut of cajoling, demonstration, value indoctrination, convincing, orientation, advice, counselling and on-the-job coaching."[18]

Many Malays went into business without knowing exactly what they wanted to do, with inflated ideas about a feasible scale of operations and with grandiose notions of what levels of status expenditure (on autos, office furnishings, etc.) the business could bear. Two easy options were often chosen. One, if the opportunity arose, was to join a company as a director, with only minimal duties. The other was to obtain a licence, quota, or contract, by virtue of being a Malay; let non-Malays run the business; and take a percentage of the profit. Such arrangements, especially common in mining, timber, or saw-milling, were known as "Ali Baba"—with Ali denoting the Malay, and Baba (originally a name for "Malayized" Chinese in the Straits Settlements) denoting the Chinese. It was said that in 1979 one such business in Kedah, although nominally Malay, actually kept its accounts in Chinese!

Yet, in spite of these difficulties, some progress has been made. The number of businesses owned by Malays, or other indigenous people, increased from 14 percent of the total in 1970 to 25 percent in 1980.

If greater Malay participation in business had been wholly dependent on the growth of small-scale Malay entrepreneurship, economic restructuring would not have proceeded very far by 1990. However, this was not the only way in which the Malay component in the economy could be increased. The chosen instruments were government corporations and other similar bodies. Some were already in existence, but others, such as PERNAS, were new; each state also had a State Economic Development Corporation (SEDC). These bodies served NEP objectives in several ways. They employed mostly Malays. They provided services for Malays in business, such as making premises available, selling them goods wholesale, and giving them loans, advice, and so on. They had the great advantage of being able to provide training for Malays in the practice of management, although such training would not necessarily equip them for entrepreneurship, in which a higher degree of successful risk-taking is required and in which there is more exposure to market forces. Certain of these government corporations, notably PERNAS, had a whole network of subsidiaries (some reaching down as far as a fifth "generation") that took the form of joint ventures with foreign firms, thus making it possible for Malaysia to obtain some of the benefits of advanced technology. The number of corporations, boards, and institutes is staggering; including subsidiaries, the total is more than a thousand. Their names alone, often referred to by initials, constitute a verbal jungle.

The range of activities covered is vast. PERNAS and its sixty or more subsidiaries and associated companies engage, among other things, in trading, mining, property development, and securities. The SEDCs operate in agriculture, manufacturing and processing, shipping, hotels, wholesale and retail trading, and so on. At the same time, however, the number and complexity of the operations of these bodies bring with them corresponding disadvantages, such as the tendency to overexpand and the problem of how to apply controls so as to check inefficiency and dishonesty without cramping initiative. The most appalling case of inadequate supervision concerned Bumiputra Malaysia Finance (BMF), a wholly owned subsidiary of Bank Bumiputra (previously established to help the Malays in business). In 1983, BMF lent too much money to a few Hong Kong firms that speculated in property, two of which went bankrupt when market values dropped. Three BMF officials had awarded themselves lavish "consultancy fees," and, even more sensational, a BMF official sent to investigate was found murdered in Hong Kong. Top BMF officials, mostly Malays, had been bribed by one of the firms that went bankrupt.[19] Total BMF losses were at least M$2 billion (almost US$1 billion)—about 3 percent of Malaysia's national income. There were rumors (not substantiated) of the implication of Tengku Razaleigh, formerly the chairman of Bank Bumiputra and, in 1983, minister of finance with power of direction over the Central Bank, which in turn has legal powers over Bank Bumiputra. A glaring example of inefficiency concerned a subsidiary of RISDA (the Rubber Industry Smallholder Development Authority), which, in an effort to help smallholders, bought some Korean crockery that was so unsalable that it actually had to be given away. Over half the companies in which SEDCs invested ran at a loss; some were so inefficient that, starting in the late 1970s, the government closed them down. Many of these organizations' activities were intended to be temporary, and it was stated that in due course they would be transferred to the private sector.[20]

Malay Ownership of Wealth: Corporate Assets

The NEP also made provision for increasing the Malay proportion of wealth, with an emphasis on the ownership of corporate assets through shares. Although Malay participation in the economy is a "passive" contribution compared to entrepreneurship, it was the most ambitious goal of the NEP, and one that attracted much public attention. For Peninsular Malaysia, Malay ownership (by Malay institutions as well as Malay individuals) of corporate assets was only 2 percent of the total in 1970, whereas the non-Malay share (almost entirely Chinese) was 34 percent and the foreign share more than 60 percent. The 1990 target specified that the proportions should be 30 percent, 40 percent, and 30 percent, respectively. To attain the higher Malay proportion, two main conditions had to be met. First was the legal requirement that businesses should increase the Malay holdings up to an average of 30 percent by 1990, which was enforced through the licensing provisions of the Industrial Coordination Act. Second, there had to be a larger *supply* of Malay capital. Somehow the relatively poor Malays had to increase their savings spectacularly, but, quite apart from poverty, many Malays were inhibited from buying shares because the idea was so novel to them.

Just as with the previous problem of how to create Malay entrepreneurs, part of the solution was to invoke the aid of government-type bodies by counting the shareholdings of agencies such as PERNAS as being held "on behalf of" the Malays. As the plans progressed, something like four-fifths of "Malay" ownership assumed this form. This type of ownership was not entirely fictitious; quite poor Malays who visited the Hilton Hotel in Kuala Lumpur (partly owned by PERNAS) were heard to refer to it as "our hotel." A drawback, however, was that the shares purchased by these bodies had to be paid for by the government, thus imposing a strain on expenditures, which became hard to sustain during the economic recession of the early 1980s. In addition, the government set up a number of unit trusts to tap the savings of those individual Malays who were able to save, if they could be persuaded to do so, but who were still not rich. The most important of these is now the National Unit Trust (Amanah Saham Nasional). The number of units an individual may hold is limited, and units can only be sold back to the Trust, not to rich Malays or to non-Malays. Partly because of the recession, Malay corporate ownership, achieved by both these means, is behind schedule. In 1980, the percentage was only 12 percent, instead of the target of 16 percent. By 1983 it had increased to 18 percent, but the 1990 objective of 30 percent seems unattainable.

Malays in Higher Education

No targets were set for increasing the proportion of Malays in higher education, although such an increase was clearly a precondition for successfully restructuring society. In 1970, Malays were represented in short nondegree courses more strongly than was indicated by their numbers in the population. In degree courses, however, they formed only 40 percent of the students and were very much underrepresented in science, medicine, and engineering. During the next decade, the percentage of Malays taking degree courses rose to two-thirds or more, although subsequently this percentage declined. In absolute terms, the number of Malays in degree courses in local universities in 1980 was approximately 14,000, while another 5,000 or so were in universities overseas. As before, too few Malays were studying science, medicine, and engineering. The smaller percentage of non-Malays attending degree courses locally was counteracted by the larger numbers who studied abroad.

Achievements and Prospects

The NEP drive against poverty has achieved much less than had been hoped for. Apart from the adverse effects of

the economic recession in the early 1980s, the government
for some time did not really tackle the basic issue of the
uneconomically small holdings of rice and rubber. On the
positive side, without some version of the NEP the economic
position of the Malays would be worse than it is, and the
economic gap between Malays and non-Malays would have
widened. Moreover, although the restructuring of society has
not proceeded in an entirely smooth fashion, Malaysia is to
be credited for having carried on at the same time as it
sustained a high growth rate.

As many as a half-dozen years before the target date
of 1990, these questions were already being asked: Should
the NEP continue beyond then? Should it be extended until
poverty was largely eliminated, until the Malays reached the
30 percent ownership target, or even until they achieved 50
percent ownership? Perhaps the most authoritative answer
has come from Dr. Mahathir, who in 1983 said that it should
continue until the Malays were confident that they could
compete with the other ethnic groups with comparable assets
and "from all aspects."

Reactions to the NEP

Two types of reaction to the NEP are worth noting:
those of the non-Malays (especially the Chinese) and those
of foreign investors. Given the fact of high economic growth,
at least until the early 1980s, non-Malays were not in fact
seriously squeezed economically by the NEP. In 1980 the
average household income of the Chinese was nearly twice
the Malay average, and the Indian average was one-and-a-
half times the Malay figure. However, it was hard for non-
Malays not to *perceive* the situation as one in which the size
of the "pie" was limited. They were particularly worried by
the ICA, given their concern not so much about the principle
of higher Malay participation in business but rather about
the implementation of the licensing requirements, which originally gave officials wide powers of discretion and thus made
business calculations uncertain. The ICA has sometimes been
blamed for a fall in private (Chinese) investment in the mid-

1970s, although there were other possible reasons, such as the mild economic recession and the lack of confidence resulting from the United States' withdrawal from Vietnam and Kampuchea (Cambodia). A second source of resentment was the increased proportion of Malays admitted to Malaysian universities under the NEP. This feeling arose among the Chinese because, in combination with the government's refusal to allow the establishment of a primarily Chinese university, it both represented a blow against their culture and negatively affected their future earning power. The government responded on these issues. Concessions and clarifications were made with respect to the operation of the ICA, and the proportion of Malays in the local universities was reduced.

Non-Malays were also worried that, through the creation of giant bodies such as PERNAS, the Malays would get a step ahead in business because so many Chinese and Indian firms were only small family businesses. Accordingly, the MCA in 1975 established a modern corporation with huge financial resources—namely, "Multi-Purpose Holdings," which has been extremely active but also open to the criticism that it has been too much subject to the political goals of MCA leaders. The MIC set up a modest Indian counterpart.

Many of the attractions of Malaysia to foreign investors before the New Economic Policy persisted after its adoption. The NEP still offered a wide supply of raw materials, relatively cheap labor, fewer bureaucratic obstacles than most neighboring countries, and a favorable attitude toward investment based on a predominantly free enterprise philosophy. Malaysian governments did not accept that their relationship to industrially advanced countries must necessarily be a "dependent" one. They relied on their own abilities to bargain with foreign investors on an equal footing. After the NEP took effect, requirements on Malay employment and ownership were spelled out for investors more formally than was previously the case, but still with some flexibility. Malaysia's attitude toward foreign investment was no less welcoming than before; indeed, the NEP's success greatly depended on a high rate of growth, which in turn required a high rate of foreign investment. However, the ICA did give rise to difficulties. Initially the powers it conferred on the government were very wide-ranging, and foreign firms, as well as Malaysian firms, could not be sure that their applications would meet such requirements as the hiring of sufficient Malays, having a high enough proportion of Malay shareholders, and so on. These fears were largely dispelled after Dr. Mahathir took over as trade and industry minister in 1977. However, the confidence of foreign investors was shaken by the Petroleum Development (Amendment) Act of 1975, which extended the powers of PETRONAS, the government oil organization. The act contained the ominous provision that in joint ventures PETRONAS could acquire control with very few shares through the use of special "management shares," which carried disproportionately high voting power. This provision was withdrawn, but only after confidence had been undermined for a time.

Concurrently, agencies of the government bought a share, often a controlling share, in certain foreign companies operating in Malaysia, especially in plantation holdings. These takeovers were in the open market and in no sense amounted to nationalization. In late 1981, however, the British appeared to be obstructing certain of these takeovers, which contributed to the temporary rift in Malaysian-British relations described in the following chapter.

These takeovers were complex, involving almost impenetrable networks of subsidiaries and holding companies. One of the current major Southeast Asian multinational companies, PERNAS Sime Darby, originated through the purchase of shares of a British plantation company by PERNAS. Such operations were closely linked to the objectives of the NEP. They increased the proportion of corporate wealth held by Malaysians as opposed to foreigners and, more particularly, increased the percentage of such holdings classified as "Malay."

In 1984 and 1985, in order to encourage more foreign investment, the rules about limiting foreign equity participation to 30 percent were relaxed, mainly for firms exporting a high percentage of their production or qualifying as "high technology" industries.

DEVELOPMENTS IN THE 1980s

In the early 1980s, new themes were superimposed on the NEP, although its basic thrusts remained. One such theme concerned the development of heavy industry. The others were the "Look East" policy and a policy of privatization.

The Development of Heavy Industry

The first indication of the new emphasis was the establishment of the Heavy Industries Corporation (HICOM) in 1980; the originator was Dr. Mahathir, then minister for trade and industry. In 1983, the outlines of the strategy became more clearly defined. Previously, manufacturing had concentrated on such items as the processing of imported raw materials (food and chemicals) and assembling of imported components (electronics and vehicles). The domestically added value of these products was low, the technological transfer was minimal, and the contribution to developing a skilled labor force was limited. The government's intention now was to give Malaysia the basis of an indigenous industrial technology by concentrating on heavy industrial production—for example, cement plants, iron and steel production, ammonia-urea factories, and petrochemical production. The government's determination was shown by its commissioning of several United Nations Development Program experts to help draw up an Industrial Development Master Plan by 1985 and by the fact that HICOM was exempted from the extensive cuts in Malaysian budgetary expenditures imposed in October 1983.[21] One of the proposed ventures "pushed very hard" by Dr. Mahathir was the production of a made-in-Malaysia car, to be manufactured through a joint subsidiary of HICOM and the Japanese multinational, Mitsubishi. At first, most of the components would be imported and would come into production in the mid-1980s. The scale of manufacture, even by 1988, would be only about 60 percent of the minimum thought to be economically viable, which was about 200,000 units a year. The first car came off the assembly lines in July 1985.

The problems involved in producing the car illustrate the possible drawbacks of the heavy industries program generally. Where could the products be exported, against competition from, say, South Korea or Taiwan? What would be the cost to Malaysian consumers, unless there were substantial exports, given that the car would need heavy tariff protection? A long-run solution would be to make the scale of production economic by increasing the Malaysian population, thus providing a larger market (a figure of 70 million people by the end of the next century has been advocated by the government).

The ambitious nature of some of the aforementioned projects—which require large capital outlays, joint ventures with foreign firms, and often the use of foreign contractors—will make heavy financial demands on the government. Considering the constraints imposed by the recent large increase in the deficit, the government may decide not to attempt some of the projects soon. One feature of this kind of development is closely related to NEP objectives: Because state bodies will play a major role in the development, there will be a need for still more Malay managers.

The "Look East" Policy

A striking development occurred in 1982, when a "Look East" policy was announced by the prime minister.[22] It was based on the idea that Malaysia had been too dependent on Western values and that, in any case, Western countries were no longer setting the pace materially, while morally they were becoming materialistic and atheistic. What other countries could be offered as models? As yet, China was not very economically developed. Taiwan, Singapore, and Hong Kong were more suitable, but all three were predominantly Chinese—a fact that would place obstacles in the way of Malays following their example. Japan and South Korea, on the other hand, were appropriate countries to refer to in the new policy.

Exactly what features did Dr. Mahathir hold up as worthy of imitation? Obviously, as he pointed out, it would be impracticable, and also undesirable, to try to reproduce a complete copy. Not everything in the West was wholly bad, nor was everything in the East wholly good. As an extreme example, Malaysia should not adopt the Japanese method of suicide, *hara-kiri*! To a degree, the emphasis was on Japanese technology and business techniques. But, for the most part, Dr. Mahathir repeatedly praised such Japanese qualities as loyalty, unselfishness, efficiency, cleanliness, sincerity, thrift, trustworthiness, and, above all, hard work and discipline. Efficiency, cleanliness, and trustworthiness, in particular, corresponded to the themes stressed in the Barisan Nasional's 1982 election manifesto as being desirable in government. They were also in close agreement with the campaign being carried out by the government to ensure hard work, punctuality, and efficiency in government offices and to spread such ideas through "leadership by example." The "Look East" policy had a high moral content, although it was also intended to produce material payoffs. In a way, it was reminiscent of an attempt to capture the "Protestant Ethic," in which religious motives were thought to be the driving force behind hard work and success in business. More specifically, the prime minister saw these values as being compatible with (indeed, derivable from) Islam—a relationship summed up in the government slogan, "Discipline Through Islam."

Criticism of the policy tended to fasten either on those aspects of life in Japan or South Korea that did not seem to deserve imitation or on those that would be hard to reproduce in Malaysia. Critics pointed out that human rights and working conditions were not idyllic in these countries and that, historically, Japan differed substantially from Malaysia because it had never been colonized and during the Meiji regime had been able to tax the peasantry heavily, thus making successful industrialization possible. Malaysia could not hope to reproduce this background. Other complaints referred to the experience of Japanese and South Korean firms operating in Malaysia and included allegations of arrogant behavior, discriminatory treatment, and even physical violence.

On a deeper level, some critics believed that it was inappropriate to hold up Japan as an example given that the relationship between Japan and Malaysia was one of dependence. Such attacks would have been incurred by any industrially advanced power with which Malaysia had very close relations, but Japan was particularly vulnerable because of its exploitative use of the "Co-Prosperity Sphere" idea during World War II. More explicitly, the dependent relation arose mainly because Japan was more developed industrially and needed Malaysia less as a trading partner than Malaysia needed it. Consequently, Malaysia had a huge deficit in trade with Japan in early 1984, and its dependent status was reflected by the nature of its exports, which were mostly primary products, and by the concentration of Japanese investment on resource-based and labor-intensive industries. Japan, it was said, held "three cards in one hand"—trade, aid, and investment—whereas Malaysia held only one card—trade—and even that was lower ranking, as a result of Japanese import restrictions. Other criticisms of the relationship were that it involved little transfer of technology or use of locally manufactured components. In his 1984 speeches the prime minister showed awareness of these considerations.

The "Look East" policy is being implemented by Malaysia in several different ways: through education and training schemes, through the use of trading companies on the Japanese pattern, and through the concept of "Malaysia Inc." Schemes for sending students and trainees to Japan and South Korea have been supplemented by exchanges of teachers, professors, officials, and business people. However, initially at least, the total numbers involved have been only a fraction of those exposed to similar training or exchanges in Western countries. The plan for promoting trade through large-scale companies was modeled on the Japanese *sogoshoshas*. Six of these bodies were formed by the end of 1983 and were given the task of promoting Malaysian exports, particularly exports of manufactured goods. But progress was slow to begin with, as the firms persisted in claiming that they needed incentives before they could "take off" while the government continued to insist that they demonstrate results first in order to show that they were worthy of receiving incentives.

The Malaysia Inc. idea was launched by the prime minister in February 1983. The concept was based on an adaptation of "Japan Inc.," in which the whole country is regarded as one corporation, with the private and public sectors working together to promote development. The relationship between the two sectors, the prime minister pointed out, was to be that of a partnership; the state was not to control everything. There were to be regular dialogues between representatives of the two sectors in monthly public forums. More particularly, the government was to give additional assistance to exporters, and the attitude of officials toward business was to change; bureaucratic bottlenecks were to be minimized, and the private sector's requirements were to be dealt with helpfully, not grudgingly. The new spirit of partnership was symbolized in the theme of the 1983 National Day Parade, "Together Towards Success," which referred to public-private cooperation. The private sector was also invited to contribute ideas and support to the Industrial Development Master Plan.

Privatization

Privatization, the process of handing over functions previously performed by the government to private enterprise, differs from the concept of Malaysia Inc. However closely the public and the private sectors may be cooperating, it is still important to distinguish between the respective roles of each sector. Because the concept of privatization and that of Malaysia Inc. are related, however, and because they were announced by the prime minister at about the same time, they have often been confused—even by some of the ministers who tried to distinguish between them.

The New Economic Policy, with its emphasis on the use of corporate bodies to engage in business on behalf of the Malays, had produced a strange situation. The government was basically pro–free enterprise, and yet it performed many functions that, in other countries, were carried out by the private sector. Payments to civil servants in salaries and tax-free pensions amounted to nearly 40 percent of the national income in the early 1980s—a much higher proportion than that in Thailand or South Korea. The costs of the services provided to the public had mounted, and yet there were demands for more and better-quality services. Given the increased deficit that followed the economic recession, the government could not contemplate expanded activities by bodies such as PERNAS and MARA. Financial pressures were heightened by the government's new commitment to develop manufacturing, particularly heavy industry. These factors taken together, and encouraged perhaps by trends in such countries as the United States and Britain, contributed to a new policy of privatization. However, the considerations in question were not sufficient for the adoption of such a policy. A few years before, privatization would have been ruled out for political reasons because the main benefits would inevitably have been enjoyed by non-Malays and foreigners. As it was, by 1983 it seemed likely to open up new opportunities for Malay managers while at the same time decreasing government spending and increasing efficiency. The government also saw that, even if privatization might sometimes result in higher prices to consumers, public resentment would then be directed not toward privatization but, rather, toward business people.

Exactly which activities were to be privatized? Among the functions the government was soon negotiating to hand over were the third television channel, telecommunications, shares in a MARA shipyard, the operation of facilities at Port Kelang (the port of Kuala Lumpur), and the Malaysian Airlines System (MAS). Shares amounting to 30 percent of the MAS capital were offered for sale in October 1985. Other probable choices for privatization were electricity, part of the railroads, the postal service, some stretches of the road system, and the Malaysian International Shipping Corporation.

The government was not doctrinaire about applying the concept of privatization. It announced that it would look at each individual case before making a decision. It also said that after a service was privatized, it would watch out for unfair rises in costs and for breaks in continuity of service— a necessary precaution as many of the functions to be handed over were monopolies or near-monopolies. In addition, it gave assurances to trade unions, which feared that workers' wages and conditions of service might be adversely affected by the change.

Some services might be considered essential, yet fail to attract any bids from the private sector. These presumably would have to remain governmental. Others, not essential but carried on by such bodies as MARA or the SEDCs, would probably just be discontinued, as has already happened in some cases.

Some of the enterprises to be sold off were huge, and the amount of capital needed to purchase them would obviously be hard to raise. Such transfers might be easier to manage if the sales took place in stages, or if the government were to retain a share. Alternatively, a split might occur between the public and private sectors: The functions of the National Electricity Board might be divided between the two, or the government might continue to run existing services for the railroads while permitting the planned new services to be private. The particular problem of raising enough *Malay* capital to conform to the provisions of the NEP could be made easier by the formation of partnerships between Malay firms or organizations and foreign and non-Malay firms, thus ensuring Malay control and also qualifying as "Malay" for NEP purposes.

SUMMARY

So much of Malaysia's economic policy is so new that any conclusions drawn about it must be provisional. A few generalizations are possible, however. Since independence, Malaysia has come a long way from being a "tin and rubber" economy. The latest development, the new strategy of promoting heavy industry, seeks to encourage still more diversification but, as the experience of India in the 1950s has shown, may also encounter formidable obstacles. None of the new developments in policy—the concentration on manufacturing, Look East, Malaysia Inc., and privatization—are incompatible with the "restructuring" aims of the NEP and the need to improve the economic position of the Malays. However, all of them depend on, yet also provide a stimulus for, an increase in the number of capable Malay managers and entrepreneurs for both the public and the private sectors.

7

Foreign Policy and Security

Some leaders, when their countries achieve independence, beat their chests and shout, proclaiming their importance to the world, while their own people starve.[23] The first prime minister of Malaya, Tunku Abdul Rahman (and the author of the above observation), was in no danger of falling into such a trap. As the leader of a small country, still engaged in fighting Communist rebels with the help of British and British Commonwealth troops, he had neither the opportunity nor the wish to change the broad lines along which the colonial power had conducted its foreign policy. He was a realist who saw Malayan and British interests as coinciding closely because communism was the main enemy. Continuity was helped by the fact that the Tunku had been educated in Britain and had enjoyed his stay in that country, and the fact that the transfer of power had been orderly and not secured by violence. The main immediate requirement was not to find new policies but, rather, to recruit personnel to build up the new Ministry of Foreign Affairs.

After 1957, it was possible to identify a number of shifts in the country's foreign policy. Any choice of dates must be arbitrary to some extent, but 1964, 1970, and 1975 seem to stand out. These years correspond, respectively, to (1) the influence of *Konfrontasi* with Indonesia; (2) the scheme by which Southeast Asia was to be treated as a neutral zone, combined with a new policy toward China in conjunction with a new organization of Southeast Asian states; and (3)

153

the reactions to the Communist takeovers in South Vietnam, Kampuchea (Cambodia), and Laos. In addition, since 1981 Dr. Mahathir has put his distinctive stamp on Malaysia's foreign policy.

FOREIGN POLICY, 1957–1970: REACTIONS TO MALAYSIA

Until 1964, no really significant new directions in foreign policy had been taken. Malaya/Malaysia was a staunch supporter of the United Nations (particularly inasmuch as the UN had assumed a protective role over small nations), was sympathetic to the aspirations of other Muslim countries, and had been a vocal critic of continuing colonialism (e.g., by the French in Algeria and by the Portuguese in Africa). The Tunku was also a determined foe of apartheid in South Africa and had contributed to forcing that country to leave the Commonwealth. Even after the Communist insurrection was declared ended in 1960, Malaya made no effort to open diplomatic relations with mainland China or the USSR.

Indeed, it was rather surprising that Malaya did not demonstrate its opposition to communism by joining SEATO (the Southeast Asia Treaty Organization, designed to counteract Communist subversion), which included Thailand and the Philippines as well as the United States and other Western powers. This seeming lack of consistency is partly explained by the existence of defense agreements between Malaya and Britain, Australia, and New Zealand, by which these countries provided troops and were given bases to help fight the insurgents, thus rendering other assistance less urgent. In addition, the prime minister, who was also responsible for foreign affairs, was unwilling to displease India, China, and Indonesia, which, like many other Third World countries, were opposed to SEATO. The Tunku, however, could see that the country needed to establish friendly relations with some nearby countries in preparation for the time when the British and other Commonwealth troops might withdraw completely, although initially only limited progress was made in this direction. Malaya, Thailand, and the Philippines formed the

Association of Southeast Asia (ASA) in 1961, which made a number of agreements, on a modest scale, concerning trade, tourism, and cultural exchanges.

Just two years later, Malaya's relations with the Philippines and Indonesia sharply deteriorated as a result of the proposal for the formation of Malaysia. The Philippines, under President Diosdado Macapagal, resurrected its claim to North Borneo (Sabah), asserting that in 1878 the Sultan of Sulu had merely "leased," not "ceded," the territory to the predecessors of the British North Borneo Company or, alternatively, that he had lacked the power to transfer sovereignty. In either event, the Philippine government claimed to be the sultan's true heir. The Indonesian objection was ideological rather than legal. President Sukarno had entered an anti-Western phase and saw the Malaysia proposal as a "neo-colonialist" scheme hatched by the British, whose troops were still in Malaya, thus proving that the country was not yet really independent. There were some complex twists and turns in Malaya's relations with the two countries during 1963, the most remarkable being the proclamation of a new organization, "Maphilindo" (although its objectives were obscure and it was never actually established). Indonesia's *Konfrontasi* policy not only meant that diplomatic and trade relations had to be broken off; it also included actual aggression. There were troop clashes on Indonesia's border with Sarawak and North Borneo; bombings were instigated in Singapore; and troops were dropped or landed on Malaya's west coast. In 1966, after Suharto had replaced Sukarno and Ferdinand Marcos had succeeded Macapagal, diplomatic relations were resumed with both Indonesia and the Philippines.

Indonesia's hostility produced not just obvious direct effects, such as restrictions on Malaya's trade and higher military expenditures. It also revealed how badly Malaya was in need of additional contacts and friends. Indonesia had used international conferences to urge its case against the formation of Malaysia and lobbied so successfully at the Afro-Asian Conference held in Tanganyika (later Tanzania) in 1963 that the delegation from Malaya-Singapore failed even to get seated. Consequently, through *Konfrontasi*, Malaysia learned the hard lesson that it had to be active and to seek support in Third World organizations and forums and also needed to increase the range of its diplomatic representation. The most important early example of this latter concern was the conclusion in 1967 of a trade agreement with the USSR, followed by an exchange of diplomatic missions.

FOREIGN POLICY, 1970-1975:
A NEW APPROACH

ASEAN

A more decisive change in foreign policy occurred after Tun Razak became prime minister in 1970. The new approach was based on three related concepts: ASEAN (Association of Southeast Asian Nations), an expanded version of ASA; a policy of neutralization in the region; and diplomatic relations with mainland China. Underlying all three was this question: How was Malaysia to defend itself when Britain and other Commonwealth troops and bases were gone? When *Konfrontasi* ended, these forces were reduced, and, as a result of Britain's economic difficulties, the withdrawals were accelerated. By 1976, only a few Australians were left. These withdrawals could not be compensated for by help from elsewhere; there were clear signs by the early 1970s that the United States was disengaging from the area. The solution was to build up Malaysia's own defense forces, which rose to about 100,000 by 1983, and also to seek security by diplomatic means.

ASEAN was a weightier organization than ASA. It included not only newly independent Singapore but also Indonesia, which has an extensive territory and a greater population than the other five members combined. Brunei joined in 1984. Moreover, Indonesia's record of opposition to colonialism enhanced ASEAN's credentials as an independent grouping. However, it was not immediately apparent, when ASEAN was formed in 1967, that the organization would play a foreign policy role significantly greater than that of ASA. The first (and most of the rest) of its declared aims concerned more rapid economic growth, social progress, and cultural development in the region. Initially its economic achievements were few; according to one estimate, only about a quarter of the approved projects were implemented. The economies of the countries were largely competitive, not complementary, and steps toward free trade were likely to be disproportionately advantageous to Singapore, which was more economically advanced.

The second ASEAN aim, which did not receive much attention at first, was to "promote regional peace and stability through abiding respect for justice and the rule of law in the relationships among countries of the region and adherence to the principles of the United Nations Charter." ASEAN did not provide for collective security arrangements in order to achieve these objectives; the view prevailed that this would have prejudiced its image of "neutrality." Some of the members made their own bilateral arrangements for security, however.

Neutralization

Tun Razak and other Malaysian politicians had been voicing ideas about making approaches to mainland China and neutralization for some time previous to 1971, but it was only in that year that the jigsaw began to form a coherent picture. Speaking to the Malaysian Parliament in 1971, Razak mentioned the British troop withdrawal, the U.S. disengagement, and the increasing openness of China to external contacts shown by the Kissinger visit and the forthcoming visit by President Nixon to Beijing. After Razak had expressed similar ideas in various other international forums, ASEAN as a whole took up the theme and in November 1971 called for a neutral Southeast Asia "free from any form or manner of interference by outside powers." Not contained in the actual declaration, but often mentioned by Razak, was the idea that neutralization should be guaranteed by China, the USSR, and the United States. None of these countries has in fact given an explicit guarantee, although China has been favorable to the concept and the United States has been sympathetic. The USSR, however, has been unreceptive, because it would prefer a regional grouping aimed at containing China. Yet, even in the absence of guarantees, the ASEAN members can make their own contribution to neutrality by collaborating in joint projects and, above all, by resisting any attempts by outside powers to set any one member against another.

Relations with China

The mechanics of Malaysia's approach to China followed a predictable pattern: reciprocal visits by trade missions, followed by a Razak visit to China in May 1974 that resulted in the establishment of diplomatic relations. Malaysia recognized the People's Republic as the sole legal government of China, which meant that it had to break off its ties with Taiwan. Malaysia derived some obvious benefits—for example, a large increase in trade, especially in rubber exports, and a speech by Chou En-lai supporting Malaysia's proposal for "a zone of peace and neutrality in Southeast Asia." Less obvious considerations made the task of reaching a satisfactory agreement more complex. Malaysia's relationship to China is not simply that of a small power to a much larger power. A third of Malaysia's population consists of persons who have ancestral and cultural links with China, some of whom have less than complete loyalty to Malaysia. Moreover, the Communist rebels in Malaysia, and their sympathizers, are overwhelmingly Chinese and receive their ideological direction from the Communist party in China. During Razak's Beijing visit, the Chinese and Malaysian governments resolved that the "dual nationality" principle would not apply to the Chinese in Malaysia and, consequently, that those Chinese who were Malaysian citizens would have no legal relationship with China and would be ineligible to hold Chinese nationality. Malaysian residents who retained Chinese nationality were to observe Malaysian law. However, China, if it so desired, could still make use of either group's loyalties. Moreover, China's support for the insurgents in Malaysia, mainly through broadcasts by Suara Revolusi Malaya (the Voice of Malayan Revolution), had so disquieted the Malaysian government that it had previously constituted a major obstacle to diplomatic relations. Indeed, it took a leader with as strong a "pro-

Malay" reputation as that of Razak to convince the Malays that they were not being "sold short." Apparently the Chinese government gave assurances on this issue, but in spite of later representations by Malaysia the broadcasts continued, with the Chinese leaders claiming unconvincingly that this was not a government matter but a party one over which they had no control! Nevertheless, the Razak visit was of help to the Malaysian government because of its impact inside Malaysia. The meeting between the two countries' leaders was used, and shown in poster form, at the elections later in 1974 to strengthen the support of Malaysian Chinese for the government party and to sap the Malaysian Chinese insurgents' resistance by suggesting that China had abandoned them.

FOREIGN POLICY SINCE 1975: THE KAMPUCHEA QUESTION

The fall of the South Vietnamese and Kampuchean governments in 1975 led to a further turning point in Malaysian, and ASEAN, foreign policy. Would the ASEAN states collapse one by one before the Communist thrust, like a set of dominoes (to use the phrase then current)? In fact, ASEAN closed its ranks and held a high-level "summit meeting" in Bali in 1976. There was still no provision for collective security arrangements, but a secretariat was set up in Jakarta, procedures for settling disputes among member states were discussed, and long-term economic plans were laid. As stressed by Malaysia's prime minister, Datuk Hussein Onn, a major reason for avoiding arrangements for collective security was that they might cause the Indochinese states to think that ASEAN was not really a neutral organization but a military group disguised as an economic association. For a time it was hard to discern the attitudes of the Indochinese states. Malaysia established diplomatic relations with all three in 1976, and it even seemed possible that they might join ASEAN. They would certainly have benefited economically, although in the short run their ability to trade was limited by the war damage they had suffered. On the other hand, their new governments, flushed with success and convinced of the power of their ideology, could indeed have viewed the ASEAN states as "dominoes."

A delayed effect of the fighting in Indochina, which affected Malaysia more than other countries, was an influx of refugees who were mostly ethnic Chinese, known as "boat people." The number of such refugees in Malaysian transit camps at any one time reached about 75,000.

Actually, developments in ASEAN's foreign policy took a different direction, having been dictated by Vietnam's invasion and occupation of Kampuchea in late 1978 and China's reactive "punitive" attack on Vietnam in February 1979. The Vietnamese move was not just a reaction to the Kampuchean border incidents, nor was it simply an expression of disgust over the avoidable deaths of hundreds of thousands of Khmers under the unintelligently ruthless Khmer Rouge regime headed by Pol Pot. Rather, it was prompted by the Kampuchean government's hostile attitude toward Vietnam, against which it was indoctrinating its youth—an attitude that could have delayed indefinitely the accomplishment of Ho Chi Minh's vision of an Indochinese state with Kampuchea and Laos under Vietnamese domination. Correspondingly, the Chinese response was not directed at Vietnamese expansionism as such; the transfer of power to a pro-Vietnamese regime in Laos in 1975 had produced minimal reactions from China and ASEAN. To be sure, that takeover was more predictable and less obstructive than the Kampuchean one. But the invasion of Kampuchea had been immediately preceded by a Vietnamese agreement with the USSR. Moreover, among the numerous refugees who fled after the invasion (mostly to Thailand) were a number of ethnic Chinese. For China, these events must have represented a continuation of the previous pattern of Vietnamese ill-treatment of Chinese after South Vietnam fell in 1975.

The invasion distressed the ASEAN states for several reasons. In spite of the acknowledged frightfulness of the Khmer Rouge government's policies, it conflicted with the idea that a country's government should not be removed by outside intervention and seemed to show that Vietnam was less interested in economic development than in military conquest. It also provided a frightening demonstration of the use of Soviet military aid in the region. Paradoxically, it resulted in united condemnation by the ASEAN states while bringing out differences among them on the question as to which was the greater threat, Vietnam or China. Singapore and Thailand belonged to the former group, inasmuch as the Thai position was being reinforced by its historic opposition to Vietnam, by Vietnamese infringements of its border, and by the pressures of large numbers of Khmer refugees. Malaysia (and Indonesia) considered China the greater threat, for the same reasons that had made Malaysia reluctant to enter into relations with China before 1974—namely, its own large Chinese population and China's continuing support for Malaysia's Communist rebels. Malaysia and Indonesia were also hopeful about the possibility of detaching Vietnam from its close association with the USSR. Nevertheless, both countries expressed their willingness to help Thailand in case of Vietnamese aggression. By early 1984, Indonesian and Vietnamese representatives were exchanging views on the Kampuchea issue, and the other ASEAN countries agreed to a continuation of the dialogue.

ASEAN's responses were more successful politically than militarily. Starting in 1980, every annual decision in the United Nations on which government should occupy the Kampuchean seat has ended with the rejection of the Vietnamese-installed government. Moreover, a 1981 International Conference on Kampuchea, attended by ninety-three countries, resolved that there should be a total withdrawal of foreign troops from Kampuchea and that free elections should than be held, after which the country should be nonaligned and neutral. But how could this be achieved? How could these requirements be guaranteed, and by whom? A step toward forming an alternative government was made in September 1981, when ASEAN pressured representatives of the Khmer Rouge (although its leader, Pol Pot, kept a low profile), the former ruler, Prince Norodom Sihanouk, and one other group to declare their intention to form a coalition. The prospects of military victory by the coalition forces are dim, however, and the elements in the coalition are of unequal strength. Only the Khmer Rouge has continued any substantial guerrilla activity in Kampuchea, and only the Khmer Rouge enjoys support from China.

In 1984, the situation was largely unchanged. Malaysian and Indonesian officials held informal talks on several occasions with Vietnamese leaders but found that they had no inclination to compromise. In July 1984, however, the ASEAN foreign ministers called for the reconciliation of all Kampuchean factions, including the leaders of the de facto government.

ASEAN ACHIEVEMENTS: MALAYSIA AND THE OTHER ASEAN STATES

ASEAN's membership was broadened in January 1984 when Brunei joined soon after gaining independence. The fact that Papua New Guinea is now an "observer" (as Brunei was previously) suggests that it may become a member in the future. From time to time it has seemed possible that Burma or Sri Lanka might join, but nothing has actually come of this.

Malaysia's economic performance and policies (discussed in the preceding chapter) have been influenced by the ASEAN context. An overwhelming proportion of its trade, about 80 percent, is with non-ASEAN countries. In turn, a high percentage of the 80 percent figure pertains to developed economies that restrict trade with countries at the level of development of Malaysia and its ASEAN partners—for example, through tariffs on such commodities as garments and wood products. The consultations, or "dialogues," between ASEAN and the United States, the European Economic Community, Japan, Canada, Australia, and New Zealand provide opportunities for trying to minimize these restrictions. Within ASEAN, although the member countries' products are largely competitive rather than complementary, tariff barriers are being removed step by step, starting with the least important, and therefore least contentious, items. At the same time, nontariff barriers (e.g., quotas and administrative regulations) are being gradually reduced. ASEAN internal trade is also being promoted through the efforts of its members' nongovernmental groups, which vary in their degrees of organization and formality. Progress in promoting intra-ASEAN trade has been slow, however.

More ambitious, although less successful, was a scheme for joint ventures of various kinds between two or more of the ASEAN countries, but there were frequent changes in the proposals. Two such proposals approved in 1984 concerned Malaysian groups, one of which cooperated with Philippine groups on car parts and one of which cooperated with Thai groups on motorcycle components. But it was often difficult for the ASEAN countries to reach agreement on such projects. Proposed at one time, for instance, was an ASEAN auto, with different components to be produced by the various countries. It was not implemented, however, and in 1983 (as mentioned in Chapter 6), Malaysia went ahead with plans for producing its own car.

The spirit of ASEAN solidarity is evident in still other ways affecting Malaysia. Minor territorial conflicts over areas of the ocean bed or over tiny islands, which otherwise might have been dramatized, have actually been played down. The Philippines' claim to Sabah is also dormant, although its political potential is such that the prospect of permanent abandonment is highly unlikely. In addition, cooperation has been apparent in Malaysia's defense consultations and coordination with Indonesia, Singapore, and Thailand. The greatest rewards would have come from really close collaboration between Malaysia and Thailand in fighting Communist rebels along their joint border. However, the two military forces have not worked together as closely as they might have; complicating the scenario is the fact that the Thais are simultaneously engaged in adjacent areas in fighting Muslim separatists who are Thais but also ethnic Malays.

MALAYSIAN RELATIONS WITH OTHER COUNTRIES

The relations between the ASEAN countries are of importance because a primary requisite for their survival is that they should be both internally stable and sufficiently cohesive to withstand external threats. This is a difficult requirement given the imbalance of power between the combined ASEAN states, on the one hand, and the individual major powers (China, the USSR, the United States, or Japan), on the other. Even a strong and united ASEAN cannot completely change Southeast Asia's experience throughout history of being a region *to which* things happen rather than one that *makes* things happen. The old proverb still applies: The Southeast Asian grass is trampled when the "elephants" fight over it. What can ASEAN do to minimize the damage?

The impact of China and the USSR on Southeast Asia in general and Malaysia in particular has been referred to earlier. To bring together some of the main points made in this context, we might note that all the ASEAN countries have reason to fear China, if only because of the vast disparity in size, which, combined with proximity, makes it the potential *hegemonic* power, or chief "elephant," in East Asia. In addition, the ASEAN countries, and Malaysia in particular, fear China as a supporter of internal insurgents and as a potential manipulator of internal ethnic Chinese to its own advantage. Consequently, Malaysian Chinese wishing to visit China (14,000 applications were successful in 1984) are screened before permission is granted; some applications are disallowed altogether. The Vietnamese occupation of Kampuchea also revealed a divergence between the reactions of China and those of the ASEAN countries. China is hoping for a protracted conflict that will "bleed" Vietnam and, in the most favorable case, result in the control of Kampuchea by Pol Pot forces, while the Vietnamese would eventually be forced to give up the Soviet connection and reconcile themselves to Chinese hegemony. The ideal outcome for ASEAN, on the other hand, would be a non-Communist nonaligned coalition government in Kampuchea and a Vietnamese government, free of both Soviet and Chinese influence, cooperating closely with ASEAN and acting as a buffer between it and China. Yet within ASEAN, Malaysia (along with Indonesia) is relatively sympathetic to Vietnam and relatively "hard-nosed" about China. In spite of this divergence in ultimate aims, however, it would seem that China and ASEAN could work closely together, particularly if the Vietnamese links with the Soviet Union remain strong. In 1985 Malaysia adopted a policy of basing its diplomatic relations on trade links (a dollars and cents policy). As a result, ties with China were strengthened and the prime minister visited China in November 1985.

During the last few years, the ASEAN states have increasingly perceived the USSR as a threat—partly as a result of the Vietnamese-Soviet connection. A Soviet statement that it might aid insurgents in the ASEAN countries if they supported a coalition government in Kampuchea provoked a Malaysian note of protest and an anti-Soviet rally by the youth wings of the Barisan Nasional in April 1983. In addition, a reaction has occurred against the increased activity by the Soviet fleet in the South China Sea and through the Straits of Melaka—an increase made possible by the recent availability of Vietnamese and Kampuchean ports. New air bases and electronic surveillance facilities in these countries have now brought the U.S. bases in the Philippines and the routes followed by Japanese oil tankers within the reach of Soviet air power. The more prominent Soviet presence seems to reflect both a desire to fill the vacuum resulting from the United States' partial disengagement from the area and a determination to contain China. As (then) Malaysian Foreign Minister Tan Sri Ghazali Shafie observed, the latter aim was likely to provoke a corresponding Chinese countereffort, precisely the kind of Great Power confrontation that ASEAN is most anxious to avoid in the region.

Malaysia's relations with the United States are good. In spite of the Malaysian commitment to neutrality, there are three main reasons why, in practice, the country and its people have more in common with the United States than with the USSR. First, Malaysia believes in free enterprise (as indicated in the previous chapter). Second, since the United States withdrew from Indochina, it has not "meddled" in the region, as the USSR has done in supplying aid for the Vietnamese invasion of Kampuchea. Third, the two countries are linked by the rapid increase in the number of Malaysian students in the United States, from about 7,000 to 20,000 between 1980 and 1983. The main obstacles to an even better relationship are largely economic. Malaysia, like the other ASEAN countries, would like to see an increase in U.S. investment and mutual trade. It also believes that the United States is insufficiently aware of the effects of the "waves" made by some of its economic policies in relation to smaller countries. On a general level, it would like the United States to play a bigger role in "North-South dialogue." More specifically, it objects to U.S. protectionism, via tariffs and other means, and to the effects of General Services Administration tin sales on the prices that Malaysia can obtain for this major export. Politically, too, Malaysia has some apprehension about the closeness between the United States and China, particularly given the sale of arms by the former to the latter. This is understandable, inasmuch as Malaysia remains concerned about China's growing dominance in the region.

For Malaysia, as for other ASEAN members, the relationship with Japan is ambiguous. The "Look East" policy provides an additional complication; although it primarily reflects Malaysia's desire to follow Japan's example irrespective of purely material transactions, it has also been accompanied by closer economic ties. Japan's share of Malaysian trade and foreign investment makes these ties highly important, but it also brings into focus the specter of economic dependence. Malaysia's relationship to Japan, the dominant economic power in the area, closely resembles the economic relationship between many Latin American countries and the United States. Japan did provide aid, from which Malaysia benefited, to support the ASEAN scheme of concentrating the production of a particular product in each country, although, as mentioned earlier, the project did not proceed very smoothly. Malaysia has been unhappy about certain of the terms of Japanese aid, as well as skeptical about the extent to which Japan will open up its market to additional Malaysian products. Moreover, if Japan and China cooperate more closely, will not some investment go to China at the expense of the ASEAN states? These economic fears are reinforced by the heritage of ill-will resulting from the Japanese occupation of Malaysia and combine to form a pervasive image that "Japan wants to dominate." This image, in the most serious case, could also have a military component; possible scenarios might include expansion of Japanese forces beyond the needs of self-defense, a U.S.-Japan agreement by which Japan would take over main responsibility for defense in the region, or a U.S.-Japanese-Chinese military entente.

Malaysia's connections with Britain, the former colonial power, grew weaker, chiefly as a result of the increased importance attached to regional ties (mainly via ASEAN) and to Britain's decline as a political and economic world power. Britain, too, had shifted to a more regional focus when it joined the European Economic Community in 1973. Malaysian-British relations actually deteriorated late in 1981. The new prime minister, Dr. Mahathir, was less uncritically pro-British than his predecessors. The immediate causes of the coolness between the two countries were a rise in university-level student fees in Britain, which affected the 13,000 or more Malaysian students there, and the Malaysian government's feeling that the British had tried to obstruct legitimate takeovers in the open market of British firms by Malaysian government organizations. Good relations were restored early in 1983 when Dr. Mahathir, visiting England to attend his son's graduation in computer studies, met Margaret Thatcher, the British prime minister. In the meantime, however, the Malaysian government had followed a "Buy British Last" policy by which preference was given to imports from other countries, thus causing a drop in Britain's exports to Malaysia worth perhaps US$50 million.

Relations with other countries and groups of countries may be summarized more briefly. Economic links with Canada, Australia, and New Zealand are maintained partly through ASEAN mechanisms. Relations with Australia temporarily deteriorated in 1983, however, when the new Labor government there resumed aid to Vietnam and failed to support the ASEAN stand on Kampuchea. Malaysia has suggested that the role of the Commonwealth generally, which is becoming increasingly hard to determine, might include a vigorous effort to promote "North-South" cooperation—that is, cooperation between more developed and less developed members.

168   FOREIGN POLICY AND SECURITY

Under Dr. Mahathir, Malaysian interest focused on a
new area, but one that constitutes a logical extension of
ASEAN—the South Pacific. Visits were exchanged and provisions made for economic cooperation with several of these
countries, notably Fiji and Papua New Guinea. Diplomatic
ties were also established with the new states of the Solomon
Islands and Vanuatu. At the same time, existing relationships
were strengthened, sometimes with a change in emphasis.

Active in the Nonaligned movement, Malaysia stressed
two new themes in 1983: the need to preserve the credibility
of the movement, which had suffered from its use by some
states as a means to promote Soviet interests, and the need
for wide international agreement over the joint exploration
of Antarctica and exploitation of its resources. In view of the
increasingly important role of Islam, it was not surprising
that contacts with Muslim countries and institutions were
reinforced. In 1983, Pakistan became the largest single buyer
of Malaysian palm oil. Moreover, credits were sought from
the Islamic Development Bank (formerly headed by the Tunku)
and from Middle Eastern countries in an effort to finance
projects, some of which promoted the teaching of Islam. In
the Islamic Conference organization, the focus in 1983 was
directed to the Palestine Issue, and Malaysia hosted the United
Nations Asian Conference on the Question of Palestine,
attended by forty countries, which preceded the main conference held in Geneva later in the year. At the same time,
support for Islamic nations in general was accompanied by
a policy representing an effort to tone down the effects of
the Iranian revolution.

THE COURSE OF MALAYSIAN FOREIGN POLICY

Although critical turning points occurred during the
period 1957–1984, the development of Malaysian foreign policy
is relatively easy to summarize. In 1957, the main threat to
the stability, even the existence, of the state was internal
rebellion, although it had indeed been aided by external
support. To combat this internal rebellion, Malaysia required
the help of military forces from Britain and other Common-

wealth countries. By 1984, although a Five-Power defense arrangement (with Singapore, Britain, Australia, and New Zealand) was still in being, the only foreign troops in Malaysia consisted of a tiny Australian Air Force contingent. In essence, military pacts had been replaced by diplomacy, which had invoked "neutralization"; had attempted to secure it by promoting a regional balance of power; and had won for Malaysia the friendship of a large number of countries through ASEAN, the Nonaligned movement, the Islamic Conference movement, the Commonwealth, and so on. An essential element in the new strategy was that Malaysia had to be able, through its own efforts, to maintain internal peace and stability, as it was not able to do in 1957. The last section of this chapter in therefore devoted to the internal security question.

INTERNAL SECURITY

At the peak of the Communist insurgency in the 1950s there were almost 10,000 rebels and an unknown, but certainly much larger, number of sympathizers. By the time of independence (1957), the rebellion was virtually over, but its termination was not officially declared until 1960. Even then, however, Communist activity continued, though on a reduced scale, and it flared up on two occasions in the 1970s. Terrorists returned to Sarawak from across the Indonesian border in the late 1960s and reached a strength of about 700 a few years later. Government forces fought back, and about three-quarters of the rebels surrendered in 1974. A year later, Communist attacks in Peninsular Malaysia shifted to the urban areas, and, among other incidents, an attempt was made to destroy the National Monument, which commemorated the defeat of the rebels during the Emergency. Several attacks on police officers in urban areas also occurred.

By 1984, estimates of the number of insurgents, who were drawn from Thai as well as Malaysian nationals, ranged from less than 2,000 to more than 3,000. The majority operate on the Malaysian-Thai border. Most look to China for support, which is mainly provided through radio broadcasts, although a few are followers of the Soviet Union. Three major groups of armed Communists have been identified, the strongest being the MCP (Malayan Communist party), which from 1980 on also tried to operate through a "United Front." The other two main factions were weaker, but they consolidated their strength by uniting in 1983.

Government military operations against these groups have been conducted by the armed forces, the Police Field Force, and Area Security Units, which are locally recruited but led by police officers. All depend for intelligence about enemy activity on the Special Branch of the police.

The military campaign is complemented by two other means, one repressive and the other developmental. The Internal Security Act, which existed in a different form under the British, provides for detention without trial of persons suspected of being militant Communists or subversives. This act has been criticized by human rights supporters because of its use, in the past, against some persons who did not fall into these categories (e.g., opposition politicians, including Fan Yew Teng in June 1985) and because of harsh conditions imposed on detainees and limited appeal procedures. The numbers in detention have been much reduced in the last half dozen years. To encourage development and to counter Communist activity, an attempt has been made to improve conditions on the troubled Thai border by undertaking socioeconomic projects in conjunction with the Thai government, one of the largest of which is supported by Australian aid.

Although counterinsurgency is still important, it is no longer given the same high priority as before. In 1981, the Malaysian government announced that 75 percent of the training of the rapidly expanding army would be concentrated on conventional warfare and only 25 percent on counterinsurgency. This change illustrates the success of the government's campaign against the rebels. At the same time, it reflects Malaysia's need, as a member of ASEAN, to make preparations against possible expansion by Vietnam (which is backed by the USSR) or China in the absence of any complete guarantee of protection provided by "neutralization."

8
Conclusions

The aim of this chapter is to bring together some leading themes and to suggest possible trends. Four principal headings stand out: economic achievements and problems, ethnic divisions, culture and national unity, and the nature of state rule in Malaysia.

ECONOMIC ACHIEVEMENTS AND PROBLEMS

Malaysia's economic performance has been superior to that of most developing countries. In addition to benefiting from the exploitation of natural resources—of late, mostly in the form of oil and natural gas—governments have also been ready to diversify, as in the switch from rubber to palm oil and, more speculatively, the plans to concentrate on heavy industry. In spite of government criticisms of the protectionism of Western countries and Japan, the effects of such diversification on Malaysia, although appreciable, have not been crushing. Malaysia's relative affluence may be judged on the basis of two items that appeared on opposite pages of the same day's newspaper in the 1980s. In the first, a deputy minister, acting on behalf of UMNO, presented a sports car donated by Mitsubishi, which was auctioned for US$25,000 as a contribution to the cost of the party's new building complex. In the second, employers of domestic servants were given the good news that they no longer needed to take on inexperienced people straight from the *kampung;* intensive training courses were now being offered to improve these people's contributions to city living.

171

Some clarification is needed to relate to each other the various components of economic policy, which multiplied under the Mahathir administration. The New Economic Policy still provides the framework. The "Look East" policy and Malaysia Inc. are best seen as dramatic ways of stressing the need for discipline, hard work, and other associated values. The privatization policy cannot be understood unless it is recognized that, in spite of the large role played by government in the economy, the country never was "socialist." State organizations were intended to advance the cause of economic nationalism and to prepare Malays for playing a larger part in business. The economic recession of the 1980s provided the impetus for the government to reduce its commitments by handing over certain functions to the private sector with some assurance that there were now sufficient Malays available to run them, in various patterns of cooperation with non-Malays and foreigners. Privatization also fits in well with the idea of placing more reliance on the market and with the policy of reducing subsidies, which the government believed were disincentives to effort and self-help.

As indicated earlier, some formidable economic problems remain: (1) finding employment, especially for graduates, and probably in the future for those displaced from agriculture; (2) the possibility that economic inequality, particularly among Malays, may increase, perhaps leading to confrontation between "haves" and "have-nots"; and (3) reducing poverty, especially in the rural areas. Linked to poverty is the "quality of life" issue. To be sure, there have been great improvements in health care, provision of services such as water, electricity, and so on. But there has also been a deterioration of living standards in some town areas where rural newcomers have arrived; these individuals are often unaccustomed to living in close proximity to others and to the civic constraints needed for sharing communal facilities. A great, widely publicized social evil now affecting the quality of life is the prevalence of drug taking. In 1983 there were 95,000 known "dadah" (cocaine and morphine) addicts. In spite of heavy prison sentences for users, death sentences for traffickers, and extensive rehabilitation programs, the number of addicts has continued to grow.

ETHNIC DIVISIONS

Breaking down ethnic divisions by a policy of rapid assimilation is just not practicable; the resistance of the non-Malays would be too strong. Nor do the Malays themselves welcome such a policy of assimilation. They wish to retain their ethnic identity and not to dilute it by the admission of others, even of Muslim converts, with the exception of indigenous people in Sarawak and Sabah. As far as language is concerned, barriers have been significantly eroded by the spread of *Bahasa Malaysia.* However, the recent emphasis on the *Jawi* script in education will impose another hurdle for non-Malays.

It will be a very long time, indeed, before life in Malaysia can proceed without constant reference to ethnicity. Currently, such questions as the following are relevant: How can "peaceful coexistence" be achieved in the context of the increasing contacts between ethnic groups, often competitive in nature, which arise from modernization and urbanization? How can government recognize the existence of ethnic divisions without strengthening them (e.g., as in the New Economic Policy)? How can it promote common values that will stretch over the ethnic divide?

Clearly, Malay hegemony is here to stay for some time. Until the Malays feel that they have reached at least economic equality, other ethnic groups will not receive proportionate allocations in civil service positions, land schemes, and the like. They will still obtain *some* allocations, however, and there will be some bargaining and compromise, as shown, for instance, in the recent improved allocations of places in university-level institutions for non-Malays. Malay leaders are willing to grant some concessions in order to make government more legitimate. Non-Malays, especially the Chinese, tend to acquiesce in a situation they consider tolerable when that situation is not "ethnically stratified." In other words, the existence of two groups—one of which exercises political, economic, and other kinds of power while the other group lacks any important source of power—is not clearly defined in Malaysia (as it is in South Africa). In spite of the operation of the New Economic Policy, the Chinese are still, on the whole, better off than the Malays.

The main threat to the existing system would probably come from attempts to impose some features of an Islamic state (more easily accepted in a country composed almost entirely of Muslims) on the whole population of Malaysia, 47 percent of which is *not* Muslim. The government apparently has this point in mind; the introduction of measures to create the Islamic University, the Islamic Bank, and so on has been accompanied by statements that the rights of non-Muslims will be respected. At first sight, it seems curious that in Indonesia, where the proportion of Muslims is much higher and the proportion of Chinese much lower, the government is less subject to the influence of Islamic movements than in Malaysia. But upon reflection, it is clear that one important ingredient in the Indonesian situation is that the percentage of Chinese is so small that they constitute no threat. In Malaysia, on the other hand, the larger Chinese and Indian presence makes Islam an obvious rallying point (in extreme circumstances, even a last bastion) for Malays who feel they are on the defensive.

CULTURE AND NATIONAL UNITY

Short of outright assimilation, is it not possible for a multiethnic culture to evolve in such a way as to constitute the basis for national unity? Surely an emphasis could be placed on the common elements among the various cultures involved, such as the importance of the family, dislike of greed and corruption, and respect for virtuous leadership. The government does indeed recognize the need for a national culture, but it also insists that this culture should be founded on indigenous (Malay) culture, including Islam, and that it should contain some elements of other cultures as well. Cultural policy, therefore, resembles language policy: One

The grand parade in Kuala Lumpur, during celebrations on Malaysia's National Day. Children and adults of the various ethnic communities, attired in colorful dress, march together past the Sultan Abdul Samad building, opposite the historic Selangor Club grounds. On the grandstand is the previous *yang dipertuan agung*, and behind him are members of the federal cabinet. (Courtesy of the Ministry of Information, Malaysia.)

element is accorded primacy, but the others are also given a place.

A problem of Malaysian national culture defined in this way is that many of its symbols, such as the *agung* and the New Economic Policy, naturally appeal more readily to Malays than to others. Non-Malays are particularly sensitive on certain points. The Chinese largely accept current language and education policies, but on some issues their reactions are understandably emotional. They resent the procedures that obstruct their ability to obtain approval for the performance of traditional lion dances (Malay resistance derives from the alien nature of the animal, which is not native to Malaysia). More seriously, they are almost perpetually concerned about the disputes over Chinese burial grounds (as in the 1984 protests against the commercial development of the historic Bukit Cina site in Melaka, which 500 years previously had

reputedly constituted an example of Malay-Chinese cooperation). In addition, although in principle they concede the
Malay claim that many Islamic values are of universal application, non-Malays still fear the prospect of "creeping
Islamization," even when they have no clear idea of what it
would entail. They are naturally most unhappy about those
circumstances in which both cultural sensitivities and economic
interests are at stake, as they were in the ill-fated Merdeka
University proposal.

The arts are not exempt from the tensions that arise
from trying to find an acceptable balance among various
ethnic elements. In drama, for example, some playwrights
have sought to "decolonize" the repertory by promoting an
"Islamic theatre," while others, although not opposed to Islam,
have resisted such a tendency. Reactions against the influence
of foreign films have also occurred, but the main alternatives
have been Malay films appealing mostly to unsophisticated
rural audiences. A refreshing exception was a recent film
with a truly Malaysian appeal—*Mekanik*—which aimed at
educated Malay and non-Malay audiences and defied taboos
by humorously presenting the quirks of various Malaysian
ethnic groups.

Because old buildings or monuments are absent in Malaysia, architects after independence (or those who commis-
sioned them) had no existing models dating from the past
to inspire them. Initially, their creations (e.g., the Parliament
Building and the National Monument) were not markedly
nationalist in style. Later, however, they tended toward the
use of traditional Malay and Islamic imagery, particularly in
roofs and arches. The Bank Bumiputra building and, understandably, the National Mosque, are good examples of this
style. Competitions for designing archways have become the
rage, featuring Malay (often Islamic) themes from mosques,
stars and crescents, the *keris* (Malay knife), Minangkabau
(Negeri Sembilan) roofs, and so on. Yet, according to some,
the use of such symbols has been rather unselective. Complaints have been made about the attempts of certain bu-
reaucrats to promote a sense of national identity by "simply
fiddling with the shape of a roof."

In contrast, favorite Malaysian sports such as soccer, badminton, and hockey provide for competition between teams representing the various Malaysian states or Malaysia against other countries, thus contributing to cooperation among the various ethnic groups.

Another aspect of national unity concerns integration between Peninsular Malaysia and the states of Sarawak and Sabah. Ethnic considerations do play some part in this process, but the main problem is to improve communications of all kinds, physical movement, news, ideas, and so on. In the absence of effective communications, these two states might not catch up, either socially or economically, with the rest of Malaysia for another two generations or so.

THE NATURE OF STATE RULE IN MALAYSIA

There are some undeniably democratic elements in the way Malaysia is governed, notably regular elections and a degree of intraparty democracy in UMNO. But authoritarian elements are also present, as in the control of the media and the existence of preventive detention. The power of the executive (shared with the ruling party and especially UMNO) is overwhelming compared with that of Parliament, the opposition, or even the courts. The main check to that power lies with the *agung*. Unfortunately, the 1983 dispute about how the check should operate threatened the delicate formulation of royal power in the constitution, which attempted to reconcile the claims of tradition and the requirements of modernity.

The Societies Act indicates that, in general, interest groups are distrusted and participation in politics is discouraged. The government believes, with some justification, that at the present stage of development, authoritative institutions should be stronger than participative ones. With less justification, law-making groups are seldom consulted in advance. This is regrettable because consultation could elicit relatively informed opinions, thus permitting a modest increase in participation without endangering overall government control.

One would be mistaken, however, to condemn the system as oppressive or the government as unmindful of the needs or complaints of ordinary people. The government is paternalistic and, when possible, prefers education and persuasion to coercion. Not only is the military securely under control, but, in contrast to certain neighboring countries, political opponents need not fear violence or assassination from government or quasi-government agents. The government is aware that the most promising foundation for stability is legitimacy, and partly through its relative effectiveness and a limited degree of bargaining among leaders of ethnic groups, it has substantially achieved legitimacy, or at least acquiescence. The main threat to legitimacy is corruption, which, although less extensive in Malaysia than in many Third World countries, persists in spite of government efforts to eradicate it. The use of money in the political process has also become more widespread, as shown in the 1984 UMNO elections, and could constitute a threat to legitimacy. The government passes two crucial tests of legitimacy and viability, however. Only a minute proportion of the population is so disaffected that it would even contemplate joining the Communists in the jungle. In addition, the transfer of power from one prime minister to another has been accomplished without dissent or disruption.

If Malaysia's future is to fulfill its promise, it must continue to accommodate ethnic divisions and tensions successfully within the new context of a resurgent Islam. It must also reconcile traditional and modern attitudes in order to maintain authority in the country, within the Barisan Nasional, and particularly inside UMNO, while at the same time permitting broad expressions of the "popular will" and responding appropriately to them.

Notes

1. Karl von Vorys, *Democracy Without Consensus* (Princeton, N.J.: Princeton University Press, 1975), 164, 205, 343–344.

2. See, for example, Diane K. Mauzy and R. S. Milne, "The Mahathir Administration: Discipline Through Islam," *Pacific Affairs* 56 (Winter 1983–1984):631–648; *The Star*, 16 July 1982.

3. David Jenkins, "Proud and Prickly Princes Finally Meet Their Match," *Far Eastern Economic Review* (February 23, 1984):12–15; *New Straits Times*, 12 December 1983.

4. *New Straits Times*, 20 August 1983. See also *New Straits Times*, 23 May 1984.

5. Suhaini Aznam, "A Failed Coup in Sabah," *Far Eastern Economic Review* (May 2, 1985):10–11.

6. *New Straits Times*, 23 April 1985; *Business Times*, 23 April 1985.

7. Suhaini Aznam, "Sabah on a Tightrope," *Far Eastern Economic Review* (June 6, 1985):14–15.

8. S. Husin Ali, *The Malays: Their Problems and Future* (Kuala Lumpur: Heinemann [Asia], 1981), 4.

9. Judith A. Nagata, "Perceptions of Social Inequality in Malaysia," in Judith A. Nagata, ed., *Contributions to Asian Studies*, vol. 7 of *Pluralism in Malaysia: Myth and Reality* (Leiden: E. J. Brill, 1975), 113–136.

10. Santha Oorjitham, "Coping Without the Young Ones," *Malaysia* (October 1983).

11. J. M. Gullick, *Malaysia: Economic Expansion and National Unity* (Boulder, Colo.: Westview Press, 1981), 249.

12. Ali, *The Malays*, 53.

13. Rashidah Abdullah, "Subordination Right Across the Board," *Far Eastern Economic Review* (January 5, 1984): 31–32.

179

14. Datin Padukah Rafidah Aziz, *Malaysia* (April 1983).

15. *New Straits Times*, 30 June 1984.

16. Through the system of "rural weightage," rural votes are counted more heavily because there tend to be fewer electors in rural constituencies than in urban constituencies.

17. *Asiaweek* (March 27, 1981), 35.

18. R. S. Milne and Diane K. Mauzy, *Politics and Government in Malaysia*, 2d ed., rev. (Singapore: Times Books International; Vancouver: University of British Columbia Press, 1980), citing a MARA report with limited circulation.

19. *Asiaweek* (January 18, 1985), 31–38.

20. *New Straits Times*, 17, 20, and 24 November 1982.

21. Mauzy and Milne, "The Mahathir Administration," 629.

22. Ibid., pp. 627–630; K. S. Jomo, ed., *The Sun Also Sets: Lessons in Looking East* (Petaling Jaya, Selangor: INSAN, 1983).

23. Tunku Abdul Rahman, *Viewpoints* (Kuala Lumpur: Heinemann [Asia], 1978), 41.

Bibliography

Ali, S. Husin. *Malay Peasant Society and Leadership*. Kuala Lumpur: Oxford University Press, 1975. An intelligent analysis of village case studies.

————. *The Malays: Their Problems and Future*. Kuala Lumpur: Heinemann [Asia], 1983. Critical of existing Malay elites, but realistic about the limited current influence of class divisions.

Aliran Speaks. Penang: Aliran, 1981. A collection of articles, addresses, and other writings by Aliran members.

Allen, James de V. *The Malayan Union*. New Haven, Conn.: Yale University Press, 1967. The best source on Malayan Union policy and the successful Malay resistance to it.

Anand, Sudhir. *Inequality and Poverty in Malaysia*. New York: Oxford University Press (for World Bank), 1983. The latest in-depth study on the topic.

Bedlington, Stanley S. *Malaysia and Singapore: The Building of New States*. Ithaca, N.Y.: Cornell University Press, 1978. An essential reference; covers Singapore and Brunei as well as Malaysia.

Blythe, Wilfred. *The Impact of Chinese Secret Societies in Malaya*. London: Oxford University Press, 1969. The most authoritative account.

Crouch, Harold, and Lee Kam Hing, eds. *Malaysian Politics and the 1980 Election*. Kuala Lumpur: Oxford University Press, 1980. Informative, although the contributions vary in quality.

Emerson, Rupert. *Malaysia: A Study in Direct and Indirect Rule*. Kuala Lumpur: University of Malaya Press, 1964. A classic, first published in 1937; compares Malaya and the Netherlands East Indies.

Esman, Milton J. *Administration and Development in Malaysia*. Ithaca, N.Y.: Cornell University Press, 1978. A case history of administrative reforms, including many cultural and political insights.

Fisk, E. K., and H. Osman-Rani, eds. *The Political Economy of Malaysia.* Kuala Lumpur: Oxford University Press, 1982. A well-documented, though sometimes repetitive, account.

Funston, John. *Malay Politics in Malaysia: A Study of UMNO and PAS.* Kuala Lumpur: Heinemann, 1980. Politics as seen from the perspectives of the two major Malay political parties.

Gullick, J. M. *Indigenous Political Systems of Western Malaya.* London: Athlone Press, 1958. A historical account and analysis of politics in the earliest developed part of Malaya.

――――. *Malaysia: Economic Expansion and National Unity.* Boulder, Colo.: Westview Press, 1981. Up to date and comprehensive; especially good on processes of agricultural production.

Jackson, James C., and Martin Rudner, eds. *Issues in Malaysian Development.* Singapore: Heinemann, 1979. Critical of the progress made in reducing poverty and lessening inequality.

Kessler, Clive. *Islam and Politics in a Malay State: Kelantan, 1839–1969.* Ithaca: Cornell University Press, 1978. A well-argued defense of PAS policies, which are often difficult to understand.

Leigh, Michael B. *The Rising Moon: Political Change in Sarawak.* Sydney, Australia: Sydney University Press, 1974. A scholarly analysis of the first troubled decade of Sarawak's membership in Malaysia.

Lim Kit Siang. *Time Bombs in Malaysia.* Petaling Jaya, Selangor: Democratic Action Party, 1978. Collected speeches of the DAP leader.

――――. *Malaysia in the Dangerous Eighties.* Petaling Jaya, Selangor: Democratic Action Party, 1982. A further collection.

Mahathir bin Mohamad. *The Malay Dilemma.* Singapore: Donald Moore, 1970. The outspoken book by the current prime minister, which was banned for years in Malaysia.

Mauzy, Diane K. *Barisan Nasional.* Kuala Lumpur: Marican, 1983. An account of Tun Razak's masterly construction of the National Front coalition.

Mauzy, Diane K., and R. S. Milne. "The Mahathir Administration in Malaysia: Discipline Through Islam." *Pacific Affairs* 56 (1983–1984). Deals with recent government policies, including "Look East" and "privatization," as well as with reactions to the Islamic resurgence.

Means, Gordon P. *Malaysian Politics*, 2d ed., rev. London: Hodder & Stoughton, 1976. A comprehensive political history, emphasizing the period 1945–1975.

Milne, R. S., and Diane K. Mauzy. *Politics and Government in Malaysia*, 2d ed., rev. Singapore: Times Books International; Vancouver: University of British Columbia Press, 1980. Largely analytical; pays particular attention to party politics and to political aspects of economic policy.

Milne, R. S., and K. J. Ratnam. *Malaysia: New States in a New Nation—Political Development of Sarawak and Sabah in Malaysia*. London: Cass, 1974. A comparison of political development and party politics in the two states.

Muzaffar, Chandra. *Protector?* Penang: Aliran, 1979. An insightful analysis of the effects of Malay "feudalism" on current politics.

Nagata, Judith. *Malaysian Mosaic: Perspectives from a Poly-ethnic Society*. Vancouver: University of British Columbia Press, 1979. A sophisticated look at ethnicity by an anthropologist, with an emphasis on Islam.

―――――. *The Reflowering of Malaysian Islam: Modern Religious Radicals and Their Roots*. Vancouver: University of British Columbia Press, 1984. A development of the preceding publication, in which the recent Islamic resurgence in Malaysia is analyzed.

Purcell, Victor. *The Chinese in Malaya*. London: Oxford University Press, 1948. The classic historical account.

―――――. *The Chinese in Modern Malaya*. Singapore: Eastern Universities Press, 1960. A compressed version of the preceding publication, extended to cover the 1950s.

Puthucheary, Mavis. *The Politics of Administration: The Malaysian Experience*. Kuala Lumpur: Oxford University Press, 1978. The best source on the social structure of the civil service and its relation to politicians.

Ratnam, K. J. *Communalism and the Political Process in Malaya*. Kuala Lumpur: University of Malaya Press, 1965. Relates to the independence period; indispensable for understanding Malaysian politics.

Ratnam, K. J., and R. S. Milne. *The Malaysian Parliamentary Election of 1964*. Singapore: University of Malaya Press, 1965. The first book on a general election in Malaysia, and comprehensive in its analysis.

Roff, Margaret. *The Politics of Belonging*. Kuala Lumpur: Oxford University Press, 1974. A good account of the ethnic influences affecting the transition from North Borneo to Sabah.

Roff, William R. *The Origins of Malay Nationalism.* New Haven, Conn.: Yale University Press, 1967. Goes deeply into the literary and other cultural origins of nationalism.

Roff, William R., ed. *Religion, Society and Politics in a Malay State.* Kuala Lumpur: Oxford University Press, 1974. An impressive concentration of research on Kelantan.

Runciman, Steven. *The White Rajahs.* Cambridge, England: Cambridge University Press, 1960. The fascinating story of Brooke rule.

Ryan, N. J. *The Making of Modern Malaysia and Singapore.* Kuala Lumpur: Oxford University Press, 1969. A reliable introduction, concise yet comprehensive.

Saravanamuttu, J. *The Dilemma of Independence: Two Decades of Malaysia's Foreign Policy, 1957–1977.* Penang: Universiti Sains Malaysia, 1983. The best analysis yet written of Malaysia's foreign policy.

Short, Anthony. *The Communist Insurrection in Malaya, 1948–1960.* New York: Crane, Russak, 1975. Not an "official" account, although it makes use of official sources.

Snodgrass, Donald R. *Inequality and Economic Development in Malaysia.* Kuala Lumpur: Oxford University Press, 1980. A thorough statistical analysis.

Sopiee, Mohamed Noordin. *From Malayan Union to Singapore Separation: Political Unification in the Malaysia Region, 1945–1965.* Kuala Lumpur: Penerbit Universiti Malaysia, 1974. Incorporates path-breaking research, particularly on the formation of Malaysia.

Suffian, Tan Sri Mohamed. *An Introduction to the Constitution of Malaysia.* Kuala Lumpur: Government Printer, 1972. Clearly written and with much information beyond the narrowly legal context.

Suffian, Tan Sri Mohamed; H. P. Lee; and E. A. Trindade, eds. *The Constitution of Malaysia: Its Development: 1957–1977.* Kuala Lumpur: Oxford University Press, 1978. A useful collection detailing various aspects of the constitution.

Swettenham, Sir Frank. *British Malaya,* rev. ed. London: Allen & Unwin, 1948. One of several books by this eminent British colonial official; essential for historical perspective.

Tregonning, Kennedy G. *Under Chartered Company Rule.* Singapore: University of Malaya Press, 1958. Covers the history of North Borneo, 1881–1946.

Von Vorys, Karl. *Democracy Without Consensus.* Princeton, N.J.: Princeton University Press, 1975. An analysis of the nature of rule in Malaysia, with descriptions of the ethnic violence of 1969.

Winstedt, Sir Richard Olof. *Malaya and Its History.* London: Hutchinson, 1958. A deep study of Malay history and culture written by a British civil servant.

Acronyms

ABIM	Angkatan Belia Islam Malaysia (Islamic Youth Movement)
ASA	Association of Southeast Asia
ASEAN	Association of Southeast Asian Nations
BMF	Bumiputra Malaysia Finance
CLC	Communities Liaison Committee
DAP	Democratic Action party
EEC	European Economic Community
FELDA	Federal Land Development Authority
FMS	Federated Malay States
GDP	gross domestic product
HICOM	Heavy Industries Corporation
ICA	Industrial Coordination Act
IIU	International Islamic University
IMP	Independence of Malaya party
ISA	Internal Security Act
MADS	Malaysian Administrative and Diplomatic Service

MARA	Majlis Amanah Raayat (Council of Trust for the Indigenous People)
MCA	Malayan Chinese Association
MCP	Malayan Communist party
MCS	Malayan Civil Service
MIC	Malaysian Indian Congress
MPAJA	Malayan People's Anti-Japanese Army
NCC	National Consultative Council
NEP	New Economic Policy
NOC	National Operations Council
PAP	People's Action party
PAS	Partai Islam Se-Malaysia
P.A.S.	Pertubuhan Angkatan Sabilullah
PBB	Parti Pesaka Bumiputera Bersatu
PBS	Parti Bersatu Sabah
PERNAS	Perbadanan Nasional (State Trading Corporation)
PPP	People's Progressive party
RISDA	Rubber Industry Smallholder Development Authority
SEATO	Southeast Asia Treaty Organization
SEDC	State Economic Development Corporation
SF	Socialist Front
SNAP	Sarawak National party
SUPP	Sarawak United People's party
UMNO	United Malays National Organization
UMS	Unfederated Malay States
USNO	United Sabah National Organization

Index